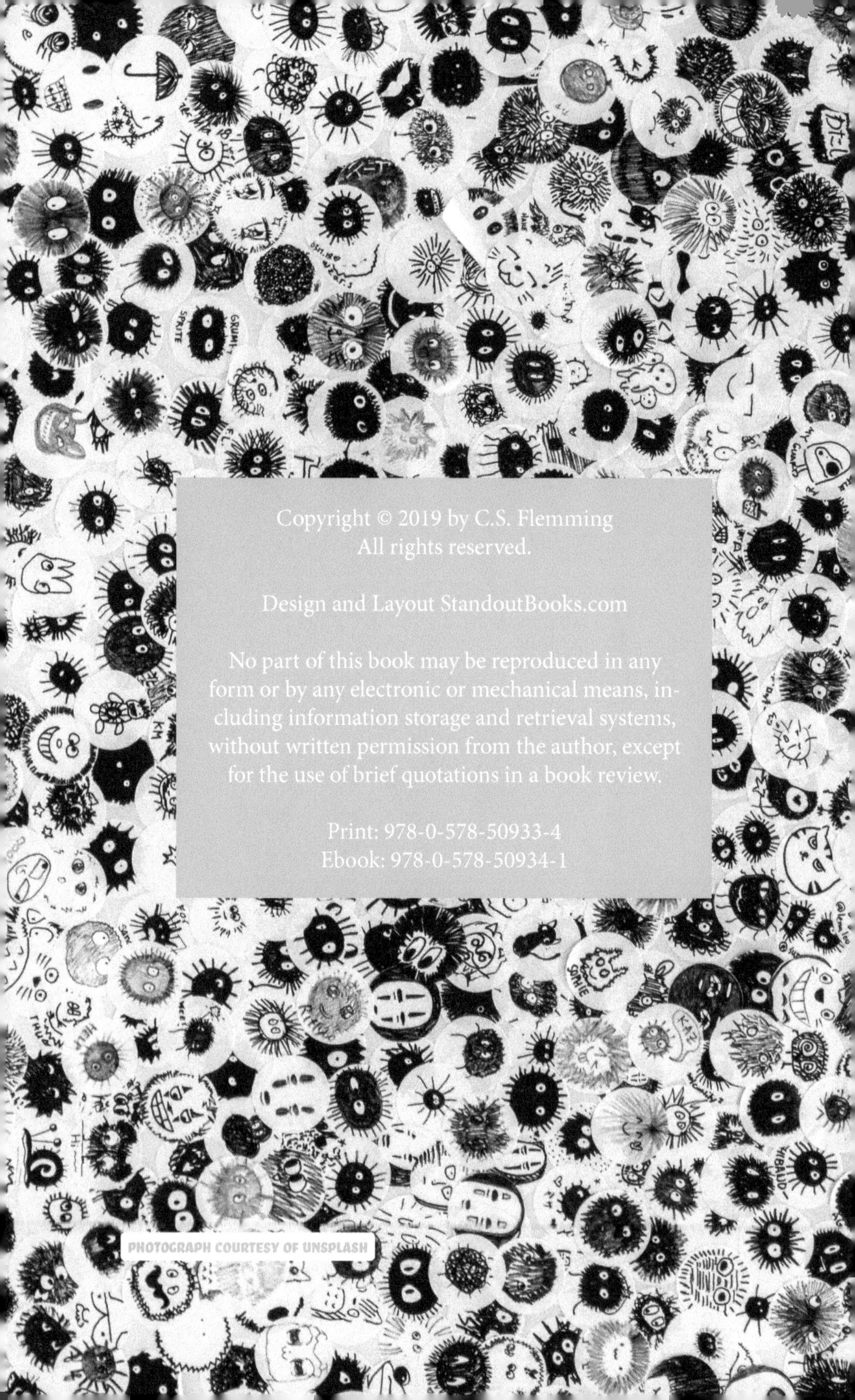

Design and Layout StandoutBooks.com

Print: 978-0-578-50933-4
Ebook: 978-0-578-50934-1

PHOTOGRAPH COURTESY OF UNSPLASH

This book and life story belongs to:

PHOTOGRAPH COURTESY OF UNSPLASH

Preface: #FinishingSchool

We are in a world that is highly influenced by societal trends, conventional wisdom, authoritative figures, and the mass media. Those forces shape, and to some extent control, our behavior, opinions, and beliefs. Sometimes they work against our ability to see below the surface and find the truth. Unfortunately, a large part of our educational system doesn't encourage truth-seeking, but rather obedience and rule conformity. This hinders many from joining the path to understanding the landscape of our modern professional world.

We no longer need to know which cutlery fork to use with each meal and how to make the perfect pot roast. Rather, today's modern professionals, especially professional women, need to be equipped with the tools, knowledge, and power to manage and navigate a landscape filled with unspoken rules, artificial and real hierarchies, a multigenerational workforce (some of whom may still believe a women's place is in the kitchen, pregnant and barefoot), variations in culture and beliefs, and modern-day bullies, including middle-school mean girls (who know how to effectively use mob mentality to keep others from succeeding and shining).

It is no longer a luxury to understand the minutiae and unspoken rules of our working environment, consisting of printer toner and cubicles. Even women like myself, who have been given the "right messages" from childhood from loving parents who encouraged us to achieve our full potential by becoming anything we wanted, find the entrance into the real world to be very jarring and discombobulating.

Most women would probably confess to spending a good part of half a decade out of school trying to figure out just really what the heck was going on. Perhaps new walls and barriers we had not ever encountered sprang up as we took our first, excited steps into the professional world. Most of us were alone, confused, and afraid to ask for help. We recognize that losing five to ten years being confused is not efficient or productive. Worse still, a young woman that discovers herself in this position may find herself in a precarious state of losing sight of her true identity and great potential. It is important to learn from your own mistakes, but we have higher hopes that you can learn instead from our mistakes and victories, as we share insight, advice, stories, and wisdom—to mitigate the time spent in confusion and fear and to instead empower you to take the next step up.

This is a time for self-awareness, a time for growth. I welcome the shifting of tectonic plates and their disruption in my life. There is no growth without growing pains; there are no islands without the chaos of two tectonic plates colliding; and there is no woman without the angry, hormonal teenage girl.

This book was written to provide a framework by which to conceptualize women's experiences within the modern professional world, to help organize thoughts, to provide support so that you are not alone, and to provide a platform to share your experiences. It is a compilation of real-life, sugar-free stories and awakening moments from both men and women, to locate organizing principles and theories that can guide us on this truth quest and make us aware of the sense of the world.

Most truth seekers start their journey when a traumatic event or experience nudges them onto the path of truth. Many of the stories you will hear include an event that awakened the writer from their slumber and made them start down their adventure of finding the truth to their lives. Each voice, just like a fingerprint, is unique to the author. It is their story, perspective, and passion. Many of the authors are sharing life insights they wish they had before venturing down their path into the working world. These are insights they not only wish to share with their own children and loved ones, but want to share with you, in hopes of making your path forward in the professional environment just a little smoother.

Despite all the modern mediums for people to share their stories and celebrations on social media, there is a loneliness that can creep in. In a world where we overshare triumphs, vacations, and puppy and baby pictures, there is a silence, a void of a deeper connection and of a sharing of all aspects of humanity, including the ability to connect on a level that allows the understanding of emotions. We tend not to share in our failures, in our struggles, our everyday frustrations. When we are faced with a fragile glass ceiling and are unable to break through, flying splat against the pane of glass, we internalize our failure, and we think it must be us, given the fragility of the glass. We shroud our failures, struggles and frustration in secrecy and bury them deep in our souls.

However, without the ability to share in our emotionally powerful experiences—the good, the bad, and the ugly—we are limited in our capacity to address the real issues. There is no sugarcoating of the experiences that you will read in this book. No story about a supermom CEO balancing childcare or marriage expertly while striking a yoga pose in her bikini on a beach in Maui.

Empathy for your stories, your life, and your experiences is most often created out of language and the support that surrounds it. Without empathy, you can't do emotions; you can't do intimacy; and you can't find the truth.

Stories are how we explain the world to ourselves and give value to the things we love. We all know how a great story at the right moment can change our minds or reveal that vital "Oh-now-I-get-it" moment.

Our goal is to continue conversations, bring awareness to topics, and raise these important issues to the surface. Sharing opens the door to connections, vulnerability, and ultimately empathy. Silence is the enemy of change and leadership, and your voice is the key. By bringing people together in shared experiences, we want to show that you are not alone and give significance to your experiences, as well as collectively provide shared strategies as we grow together in this journey. Through the weight of combined voices, the glass ceiling and stereotypes that box both men and women in will shatter.

We hope that you will share your experiences. This book is unique in which we do not pronounce the authors to be the subject-matter experts. But rather the authors are facilitators of information, sharing their own experiences in hopes that you will also share with us your stories. *We are committed to this relationship with you for the long haul.*

I share my own journey, and although my journey has had its challenges, it has been a genuine adventure. Most of my adventures that are documented in this book originated from typing on my iPhone under Notes, to document moments in time that I was experiencing and to capture the fleeting thoughts in my head. This book was meant to be raw and thought-provoking. No sugarcoating or layers of Shakespearean prose here. I don't doubt that there will be backlash, as putting yourself out there puts you at risk for criticism. People will call you out or say that you are too vocal, too aggressive, too forward, or saying too much. There is a price to pay for every push against the stereotype that you are bound in and every glass ceiling you bounce off. But there is a greater price for not breaking out of the stereotypes. Conforming can be easier and safer, but it also reinforces the status quo.

This book of lunch notes for the professional woman was created to engage the reader in sustained systematic thinking, to generate discussions, to inspire new thoughts and to provide you the emotionally powerful space to share in the truth of your own experiences. It is about a willingness to pursue the possible truth and value of ideas and the evidence for them, no matter what conclusions might result or how strange they might initially seem. A book does not always lead to truth or to ideas of great value, but it can. It often has. And the potential always exists. These lunch notes can be important to everyone because they potentially help one think deeper, more clearly, and with greater perspective.

We hope that you will share your stories with us through:

Hashtag

#LUNCHNOTES

Website

LUNCHNOTES-PROFESSIONALWOMAN.COM

Facebook

FACEBOOK.COM/LUNCH-NOTES-FOR-THE-PROFESSIONAL-WOMAN

Instagram

INSTAGRAM.COM/NOTESLUNCH

Email

LUNCHNOTESPW@YAHOO.COM

(1) #GlassCeiling

I wish I could share with you a story of an empowered woman smashing through the glass ceiling, slicing through the fragile barrier between her and success. (Insert glass shards lightly glistening off her flawless, sweat-free body.)

My story is much less romantic. It's much more seat-gripping, though, with multiple car crashes and maybe a tractor-trailer or two exploding. I promise it is more like a James Bond movie than a Jane Austin novel.

Breaking through the glass ceiling, in my experience, is more like going splat while moving at seventy miles per hour, with people rooting for you to fail as you try to chip away at the barrier, fingernails bleeding. And if you manage to break it, you'll find the glass is actually the shatter-resistant kind from your car windshield. The little crack barely spreads, held together by bonded, reinforced materials, and it is easily fixed by calling auto-glass repair. Oh, and in this case, the glass shard doesn't glisten off you, but rather it lands in your eye and maims you.

However, like a James Bond movie, my story starts off with the dramatic car crash, helicopters overhead, and a high-speed police chase. Tension builds with the formation of a highly skilled, Marine-trained war team, softens with a love story, and finishes with the good guys winning.

I hope you enjoy the journey and share with us your adventure under each hashtag, so that we can share in your joys, sorrows, angst, and triumphs. Through shared experiences, we can show that we are not alone, and we can develop empathy for each other's unique experiences. Together we can share in strategies to lessen the harsh impact against the glass ceiling (potentially reducing the impact from seventy miles per hour to twenty) and build toward a better understanding of our beautiful world.

Have you gone splat on the glass ceiling?

#LunchNotes

When did this happen, and how did it happen?

#LunchNotes

PHOTOGRAPH COURTESY OF UNSPLASH

(2) #TemperedGlassCeiling

Experiencing my first real fight with the glass ceiling came as rather a shock, given that I was apparently wearing rose-colored glasses for most of my life. Growing up with the mantra that "girls can do whatever boys can" in the nineties and being given every opportunity as a young girl to participate in everything that boys did, I was convinced that sexism was dead. There was no soccer game that I could not participate in, no university class that I was barred from, no profession out of my reach. It was a time of freedom and empowerment. I was additionally convinced that not only was sexism dead, but so was racism. My life as an "elder" millennial was going to be sweet, with barriers plowed away by the hard-working hippie women who burned their bras in the sixties.

Imagine my surprise when my first rose-colored glasses sustained a crack in the lens, and I realized that gender stereotypes and other types of prejudices still operated and had become elegantly manipulative.

These undertones were strong enough to derail women and increase their insecurities to the point that they believed their inability to crack the fragile, thin glass ceiling was due to their own failure and not due to some sophisticated, invisible manipulation technique.

Sex-based harassment typically ranks higher than all other types of harassment in the number of charges received from employees working for private, state, local, and federal employers. Based on the Equal Employment Opportunity Commission's 2016 report, sex-based harassment is consistently ranked as the most common type of harassment (EEOC 2016 report: 44%-45% alleged harassment on the basis of sex). Sex-based harassment can include gender harassment or sexual harassment. Gender harassment can be considered a "put down," while sexual harassment can be seen as a "come on."[1]

---

1 Feldblum, Chai R., and Victoria A. Lipnic. "Select Task Force on the Study of Harassment in the Workplace." Select Task Force on the Study of Harassment in the Workplace: Report of Co-Chairs Chai R. Feldblum & Victoria A. Lipnic. Accessed March 10, 2019. https://www.eeoc.gov/eeoc/task_force/harassment/report.cfm

Thus, as society encourages us to sit at the table, it is possible another hidden undertone layer exists. Thus, as the modern women bravely sits at the table, confident that she can tackle the fragility of the glass ceiling. Could it be that our adversaries have secretly replaced the fragile glass with tempered glass instead, reinforced with bonded materials to limit any damage from the assault and to prevent shattering even when rocks are thrown at it at high speeds?

Lunch Notes

When did you realize that you were dealing not with a fragile glass ceiling, but rather a barrier held down by generations-strong bonded materials? #LunchNotes

(3) #Ladder

Are you surprised if I tell you that women are still much less likely to be in leadership positions compared to men? But this is the truth, even though women have secured access to almost every profession.[2]

Ladder issues can come in three manifestations:

1. **We forgot to build a ladder.** Some sectors, such as energy, technology, and automotive and industrial manufacturing, are unable to attract women for entry-level positions, so women are poorly represented at all positions. Some ways to start building a ladder include up-front investment in female candidates to cultivate and recruit talent early on.

2. **The ladder is a stepladder.** When I first started working, right out of school, it was rather easy for me to advance. I advanced easily from a fellow position to a full-time position, then to an expert technical level. Then I got stuck.

   No matter how many additional trainings I attended, work products produced, weekend hours worked, my ladder had officially ended. No additional steps were to materialize ahead for me. The extra effort, enthusiasm, and hours worked only led to finishing the polish of the final rung on this ladder.

3. **The ladder leads to nowhere.** Unfortunately, locking women out of the C-Suite is a common issue.

2 AAUW report "The Simple Truth about the Gender Pay Gap Report (Fall 2018)." AAUW: Empowering Women Since 1881. Accessed March 10, 2019. https://www.aauw.org/aauw_check/pdf_download/show_pdf.php?file=The_Simple_Truth

Did we forget to build you a ladder? #LunchNotes

Describe your ladder that leads to nowhere. #LunchNotes

Describe your stepladder. #LunchNotes

(4) #RepeatingKindergarten

As we enter the workforce, many of us look to those mother hens or father figures to keep us under their wing. However, being coddled and told that we are cute does nothing to push us into womanhood.

When I first left school and took my initial, excited steps into the professional world, certain characteristics were reinforced, and I confess, I leaned into them because they provided me with a sense of identification in this new world.

The characteristics that were enforced included looking rather fragile and helpless and downplaying my competency and talents. Using my youth and attractiveness was an area that was also enforced; I was expected to be the pretty young fixture at the table, if I was lucky enough.

However, as I am now a parent of a beautiful, bright boy, I sometimes catch myself trying to hold onto that part of his life where he was helpless, doe-eyed, and just stinking adorable. A part of me wants to keep him repeating kindergarten, when he was so deliciously cute. However, I know if I kept reinforcing these characteristics and kept him helpless and adorable, I would be failing as a mother to encourage him to grow up to be the bright young man that I know he can be.

Then why is it, as we watch our young generation of women enter the workforce, we tend to encourage them to repeat kindergarten year after year? Reinforcing the idea that these young women are "cute"—the idea that they need protection, that it is better for them to remain helpless and dependent—does nothing to push completely capable women into womanhood and help them succeed.

So why do women stay in the place of girlhood long after it is productive for them? One of the reasons, according to Lois P. Frankel, PhD, is that we've been taught that acting like a nice girl—even when we are grown up—is a good thing. Girls get taken care of in ways boy don't.

People like girls. Men want to protect you. Be cuddly, sweet, quiet, and nice—like a pet.[3]

Being a girl is certainly easier than being a woman. Girls don't have to be responsible for their destiny and can fall within the narrow scope of expectations, namely being all sugar and spice and everything nice.

However, as per Dr. Frankel, "Nice is necessary for success; it's simply not sufficient." If you over-rely on just being nice and having other kindergarten-reinforced traits, you will never achieve your adult goals and move towards fulfillment and self-actualization.[4]

I can share from my own experience that anxiety and confusion was, and still is, part of my process of becoming more confident and courageous and embracing my power.

Lois P. Frankel, emphasis in her work, says that each time a woman directly asserts herself, she is saying, "I want something from you. I want what is rightfully mine. I expect my needs to be met also." These assertions often come with feeling guilty. We equate taking control back with taking something away from someone else.[5]

Oftentimes, the reaction we get is that we are difficult to cope with—and why can't we just be nicer and sweeter? Others don't really want the situation to change, because they already have everything they need.

---

3 Lois P. Frankel *Nice Girls Don't Get the Corner Office: 101 Unconscious Mistakes Women Make That Sabotage Their Careers*. New York: Business Plus, 2010.

4 Frankel, *Nice Girls Don't Get the Corner Office*.

5 Frankel, *Nice Girls Don't Get the Corner Office*.

Describe a time when your workplace encouraged you to maintain your "girlhood" instead of supporting you to grow into womanhood. #LunchNotes

When have you been told to "be sweeter" when you stood up for yourself? #LunchNotes

PHOTOGRAPH COURTESY OF RAW PIXEL

(5) #AcrylicGlassCeiling

Some common gender stereotypes of women include the following:

- Women are childish and helpless.
- Women are sensitive and intuitive.
- Women are scatterbrained, unstable, and irrational.
- Women can easily form deep bonds.
- Women are not primarily interested in their careers or vocations.
- Women are primarily interested in long-term relationships and parenthood.

Minority working women face another layer of glass that we tend to not talk about and just downright ignore. This layer of acrylic glass lies right beneath the glass ceiling. This acrylic glass can represent the stereotypes of an obedient Asian woman, an angry black woman, a spicy, exotic, sexpot woman, and a Latina maid.

Research has shown that minority women are at a greater risk of harassment than white women and men. This study of workplace harassment found a "double-jeopardy" situation for minority women. [6]The "double jeopardy" hypotheses describes the phenomenon that minority women face unfortunately both sexual and ethnic prejudice, putting them at higher risk of harassment. Hostility—including verbal threats, intimidation tactics, or threats of violence—is used as an effective tool to discourage minority women from entering desirable jobs. For Asian, black, and Latina women, the disparities at the top are even more extreme. According to the American Association of University

6 Jennifer L. Berdahl and Celia Moore. "Workplace Harassment: Double Jeopardy for Minority Women." Journal of Applied Psychology 91, no. 2 (2006): 426-36. https://doi:10.1037/0021-9010.91.2.426.

Women (AAUW), women of color represent less than 3 percent of board directors at Fortune 500 companies.[7]

I describe this layer as acrylic glass for two reasons.

The first reason is that the methods traditionally used to break glass (like with a hammer) do not work well on acrylic glass. The hammer likely will bounce off the acrylic glass, given the flexibility of the material, and will very likely recoil back to hit you. Thus, you are being maimed each time you tackle this acrylic-glass layer with your hammer. Different tools are needed to break through the acrylic glass—preferably a high-powered laser.

The second reason is because acrylic glass is usually not as clear as regular glass. It looks different and has a different clarity and feel—almost a translucent look. This effect creates confusion, given that the material represents glass but is not actually glass. The lack of clarity also represents a lack of clarity of the problem, as the barriers minority women face in the workforce are not well studied or addressed and are often ignored as a problem. Minority women are particularly at risk when it comes to workplace harassment. However, there is a lack of awareness or training on the issues that minority women are experiencing. Researchers and practitioners interested in issues of workplace diversity and discrimination should turn more of their attention to this very important issue.

7 AAUW report " Barriers and Bias: The Status of Women in Leadership. AAUW: Empowering Women Since 1881. Accessed March 10, 2019. https://www.aauw.org/research/barriers-and-bias/

What other stereotypes reinforce your acrylic-glass ceiling? #LunchNotes

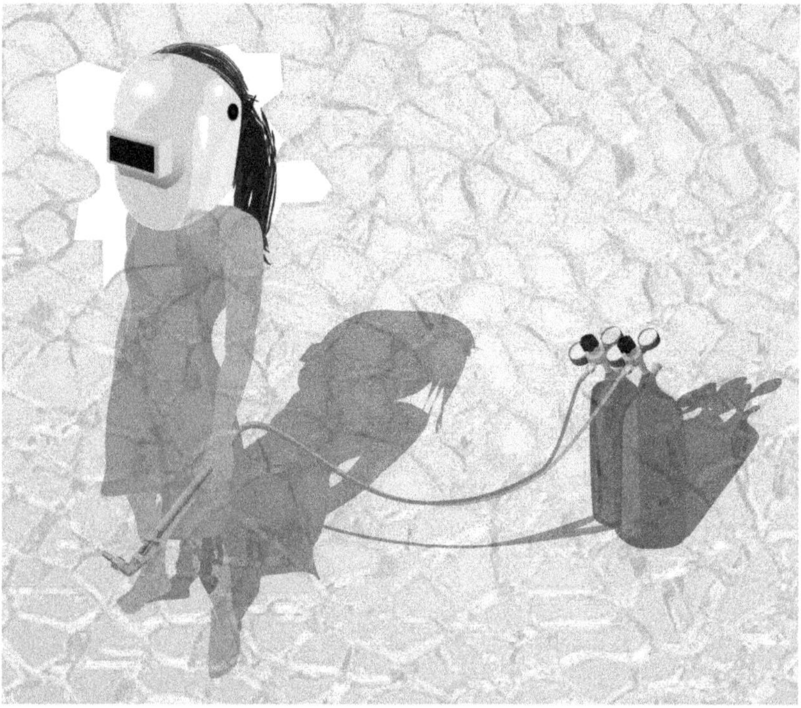

ART BY KIMBRA G. TURNER, PHD

Have you been hurt by the recoil of the "hammer" you used against the acrylic glass? #LunchNotes

This acrylic glass can represent the stereotype of an angry black woman, a submissive Asian woman, or a spicy, exotic, sexpot woman, the Latina maid. How have these stereotypes created a layer of acrylic glass? #LunchNotes

ART BY TYLER ROSENBERGER

(6) #IckyLayers

What is fascinating about this glass ceiling is that it is organic in nature. It can form additional layers of barrier-type materials depending on the choices you make in your career

Have you ever submitted to the predefined role that society has dictated for you—pretty blond in the admin role, math-savvy Asian lab technician, angry black woman—because it is too emotionally and psychologically exhausting and damaging to push against the stereotypes and because it feels much easier to just fall in line?

Or when you are asked to compromise your values, ethics, and integrity to make life easier for someone else, do you concede because it is just easier to give in? You can hear the bubbling sound of another layer forming on the preexisting layer of glass. These new layers that form are different in material, almost residual in nature. Tools that work on the tempered-glass ceiling or acrylic-glass layer (our hammers or high-powered laser guns) will not work on these materials. The only tool that works to break through these sticky new layers is the one that changes your soul and changes or denies who you are, so you can slink through these sticky, newly formed, crystallized layers.

If I did not push back on the glass ceiling when it was demanding that I compromise my values and integrity and submit to my stereotype, I would be a different person today. I would have allowed layers of icky glass to form on top of me every time I made the decision to concede and compromise on my values, until I no longer recognized who I was. Giving up little pieces of myself on my way up.

If I had compromised my values and integrity, it is possible that I would have gained some favor and through quid quo pro would have been able to cash it in for a type of advancement. However, I would have likely fallen into this habit of brownnosing and smudging ethical lines in order to survive and advance in the workforce because I would have been rewarded by a small candy every time I engaged in this behavior.

If you choose to fall into this habit, you will notice there is a counter habit that typically must form also. It is your reflex to not hate yourself. Like an elastic band, you will have to train yourself to not engage your gag reflex or to not feel the need to immediately take a hot shower to scrub your internal dislike away. Eventually, this behavior will become so natural that you won't feel icky about it any longer. It will just be business as usual. Problem solved, except for the fact that you will likely have to keep resorting to this behavior and continue working for someone who rewards this type of behavior. But, hey, if you don't hate yourself, it works.

Describe a time that you felt like you were put in an icky situation. How did you handle it? #LunchNotes

(7) #SharpTurn

There are times in your life when it becomes entirely derailed and you are forced, sometimes suddenly, to take a sharp turn. However, any turn between 1 to 90 degrees can be jarring but beneficial, just as long as it isn't a 180-degree turn that facilitates backtracking down your path.

Many times, we are happily skipping along our straight path, checking off boxes: degrees, marriage, kids, job. However, there can be times when we are forced to take a sharp turn. This could be due to a divorce, harassment, death, job loss, or bully behavior. These turns can be unpredictable and horrific. Maybe you had to make the turn because the road ahead has washed away, or a fiery car crash happened before you. This is absolutely a jarring time in your life, as you do not know whether to take a right turn or a left turn, or how much of a turn should you take (a complete 90-degree turn, or a seemingly safer 10-degree turn).

These are the types of jarring, violent, forced turns you will hear from many of the authors contributing. You will read about being pushed out of religion, the deafening sadness of divorce and loss, and the courageous sharp turn of starting a business.

Turns come many times during your life. Describe a turn that proved to be a positive. #LunchNotes

PHOTOGRAPH COURTESY OF UNSPLASH

(8) #Stereotypes

Growing up with a fierce tiger mom exposed me to my first strong female leader. The strong female role model was ever present, from making sure that my behavior was appropriate to checking that schoolyard bullies were handled with the most efficient, yet blood-curdling, manner. You all know what I am talking about.

This stereotype that Asian women were submissive, obedient, and subservient was always confusing to me, given that I was pretty sure my dad, brother, sister, neighbors, and random people in our lives did not see my independent, strong mom this way. *Submissive, obedient,* or *subservient* were never adjectives used to describe the strong female role model that I had. I have never seen anyone telling my mom to be quiet. I'm pretty sure if that did happen, the perpetrator was never seen or heard from again.

I found myself, early on in my career, guilty of playing into the stereotype that society has for women, especially young women. This included dumbing down my intellect, using the adoring-eyes method, nodding vigorously to other ideas, sitting on the sidelines, and never posing a threat to egos. These types of behaviors protected me from hostile reactions, as I abided very well by the predefined, stereotypical lines, and enforcement was never needed. However, there came a day when I wanted to grow past these preconceived lines. This is when I went splat against the glass ceiling, traveling at a lovely seventy miles per hour, and the lenses of my rose-colored glasses popped off the frame.

An additional stereotype that Asian Americans fall into is that we are good at math and science. Many may ask: How is this a bad stereotype? Unfortunately, many Asian Americans are affected by prejudice and are locked into "worker honeybee" situations with very few promotion opportunities. Statistics repeatedly point out the lack of Asian women in leadership and managerial roles. Additionally, research notes that Asian women feel that they are often neglected, forgotten, or overlooked by their workplace diversity programs or policies.[8] It is possible that Asian cultural values that emphasize sharing, being humble and respectful can be misinterpreted as a sign of weakness in the American corporate world. According to the Ascent Foundation, Asian women have lower chances of reaching the executive level than any other racial group.[9]

Another unfortunate stereotype is that Asian woman can be seen as submissive lotus flowers. Unfortunately, the stereotype of a hypersexualized, submissive Asian woman can still be an issue. The Asian fetish is not harmless. This stereotype of a submissive lotus blossom that doesn't challenge or threaten male power is dehumanizing and places Asian women at risk for harassment and violence, as they are perceived as being sexually available to men.

As such, as an Asian woman, I am dealing with three types of stereotypes:

- An underrecognized misperception that Asian people don't deal with stereotypes.
- A better-recognized prejudice against me as a woman.
- Another underrecognized prejudice against young or young-looking people. (Given that I am Asian, I will probably look like I am under forty till I reach my sixties.)

---

8 Advancing Asian Women in the Workplace: What Managers Need to Know." Report. 2003. Accessed March 11, 2019. http://wall.oise.utoronto.ca/inequity/2cat_asianwomen.pdf.

9 Deb Liu. "Finding My Voice as an Asian American Leader Meant Reconciling Two Different Models of Leadership." Quartz. June 29, 2018. Accessed March 12, 2019. https://qz.com/work/1314872/asian-american-women-are-severely-underrepresented-in-leadership-roles/.

Describe your cultural upbringing and how this influenced how you interact in the corporate world. #LunchNotes

Describe a time when your "benevolent" stereotype has limited your growth. #LunchNotes

ART BY KIMBRA G. TURNER, PHD

(9) #GlassSlipper

AURORA SKYY, PHD
SCIENTIST & RESEARCHER

The need to share stories is a basic human activity, since people do not just share stories—they live stories. As little girls, we are also told through stories about the need to fit into the roles that society is most comfortable with, and we are told that bad things can happen when we do not. One of my favorite stories growing up as an African American girl was *Cinderella*. It featured a lovely and kind young woman with a sad backstory, who was destined to triumph over circumstance by becoming a beloved princess. Cast members included a wicked stepmother, two wicked stepsisters, an absent father, a pumpkin, a godmother, a prince, cute animals like birds, and a glass slipper. I often wondered how a princess could dance in slippers made of this incredibly uncomfortable, hard, and brutal material.

In another version of the story (*Aschenputtel*, from the *Grimms' Fairy Tales*), the slipper is gold, the stepsisters are advised by their mother to mutilate their feet to fit the gold slipper, and the birds make the prince aware of the deceit. All this is done with the full knowledge that after a few steps, they will suffer pain and bloody feet. Such stories transcend culture, time, and place. As women try to fit into a delicate, yet restrictive, glass slipper, some may feel the need to arch their feet and cram their toes to fit. Often, as women, we feel pressure to fit into an unrealistic shoe and dance an unrealistic dance as we try to machete our way through the acrylic-glass ceiling.

It is inevitable that after a few steps in that glass slipper, the reality of the situation sets in. That shoe was not made for you, and it was never meant for you. It doesn't matter how much you try to fit in. You can check all the boxes that seem to work for others—having the same degrees and the same training and even changing what you wear (from dresses to pantsuits)—and it will never seem that you can fit into the glass slipper.

We see this story also reflected in corporate culture, where women, especially minority women, are severely underrepresented in leadership roles. Certain roles tend to be given to those who represent an image of those who should fit the glass slipper.

I often wonder if it is easier to just smash that glass slipper and find shoes that fit better. It could be a pair of patent-leather high heels, Birkenstocks, fuzzy bunny slippers, or combat boots (which are ideal for this battle). Or a whole shoe closet could be part of your arsenal.

As women, we have to decide which stories to listen to, and we have to write our own stories. We must gain control of whichever shoe we choose to wear, alleviating the pressure to fit into what society wants us to be.

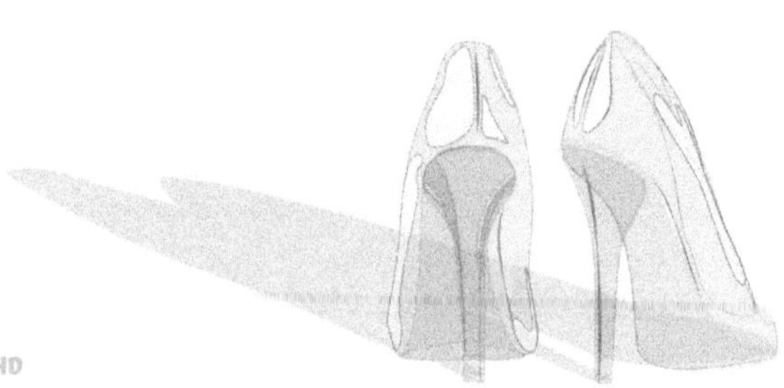

ART BY KIMBRA G. TURNER, PHD

Have you tried to fit into a glass slipper? #LunchNotes

(10) #Chingona

MK SCHIAFFINO, PHD
PROFESSOR

> *"Chingonas are the most badass girls in the world. Don't mess with them or they will kick you in the nalgas."*[10]

Sorry. So sorry. Excuse me. Pardon me. Apologies. Sorry for speaking. Sorry for thinking. Sorry for being intelligent. Sorry for loving science. Sorry for being fat. Sorry for being beautiful. Sorry for being a single parent. Sorry for being a top performer. Sorry for being loud. Sorry for saying fuck. Can we say fuck here? Fuck. Whatever. Sorry for existing in the paradigm made comfortable by someone who was not me. Yet here I was, since I was young. That time when I had to pee in second grade, and I was too scared to ask my teacher to go to the bathroom, so you all know how that ended. That time when the police stopped to help us with a flat tire when we were living in one room in LA, and all I knew was that I was sorry we had taken up space where we were not wanted, and I was so sorry our car had broken down, as if my scrawny six-year-old ass had any control over a car!

Fast-forward to a super nerd who became a magical Mexican, excelling in all things academic, always suffering from imposter syndrome, yet somehow finding joy in learning. My happy place was knowledge. I would escape into books, the wonder of sci-fi where everyone was unique and welcome, and it didn't matter what you looked like because

10 Urban Dictionary: accessed March 12, 2019. https://www.urbandictionary.com/define.php?term=chingona

we were all travelers on this spaceship earth. As I racked up accolades, I began to apologize less and embrace my legitimacy, my *right* to take up space. I looked in disdain at my mother, who continued to apologize, and I scoffed because I no longer apologized. I was empowered!

As I realized that my identity had become tied to my education, the letters after my name, the images I had associated with legitimacy, I realized I was still trying so hard to please a master who would never be satisfied, an external justification for being. I believed I was not good enough unless I was the best. This is a perspective I find to be missing with the positivity movements. It lacks the full spectrum of our being. Women are so much more than two ends of a spectrum pitted against each other as competitive "do-ers" or nurturing mothers; we are introspective, accepting, thoughtful, forgiving, and magnanimous because we *can* be. We don't have to repress the anger and rage of being discriminated against; we can experience the feeling of impotence when we've "leaned in" and no one has had our backs; and we can enjoy the pleasure of community and acceptance of our flaws and being enough. Thankfully, we can also rise to experience the transformational power of understanding that our strength is within us and that we are stronger when we let go of the identities that tie us down, realizing that we are who we are, and that is perfect. It took me forty years, and I forget sometimes, but then I drink some wine, vent, and remember. Thankfully, I have some good friends and family who remind me that I'm a #chingona #phdmom who is done apologizing and is finally enjoying all her hard work, respecting the efforts of the women who made it possible. Thanks, *ama*.

What have you stopped apologizing for? #LunchNotes

PHOTOGRAPH COURTESY OF UNSPLASH

(11) #SingleWorkingMoms

JULIETTE JOYCE, PHD
SCIENTIST & RESEARCHER

"Would you please keep this a secret between you and me?" I asked my best friend at work after revealing my single-mom status to her.

"Of course!" My friend knew exactly the reasons behind this plea: the stigma associated with single moms and the fear of losing respect and even employment!

When we think about a single-parent family, most people would instantly picture a poor, exhausted single mom with her children. And they are right. The United States Census Bureau found that about a quarter of children under the age of eighteen, a total of 16.4 million children, are being raised by single moms.[11] In addition to their traditional protective and nurturing role, single mothers often have to be the sole family providers. In the United States, 80 percent of single mothers are working, of which 50 percent work full-time and 30 percent work part-time.[12] Unfortunately, many of the jobs do not bring in enough income for the mother and her children. Single mothers are one of the poorest populations, with nearly half (45 percent) of single mothers and their children living below the poverty line.[13] Furthermore, many employed single moms are vulnerable to unemployment due to the lack of opportunities for education and training and due to the constraints of their childrearing responsibilities.

It's even more chilling that single moms are particularly vulnerable to workplace harassments. Many single moms choose to suffer in

11 U.S. Census Bureau. "Household Relationship and Living Arrangements of Children Under 18 Years, by Age and Sex: 2016." America's Families and Living Arrangements: 2016. May 04, 2018. Accessed April 18, 2019. https://www.census.gov/data/tables/2016/demo/families/cps-2016.html.

12 Wikipedia. "Single Parent." Accessed December 18, 2018. https://en.wikipedia.org/wiki/Single_parent

13 US Census Bureau, "America's Families."

silence because they have nowhere to turn and because they are afraid of losing the only income to provide for their children.

Very often, we hear some not-so-kind comments at our offices, such as, "You know that she is a single mom, don't you?" There are often no follow-up comments or explanations after this sentence. However, both parties seem to completely understand the meaning of this comment. To them, "single mom" equals being late to work, taking a lot of sick leave, performing poorly, being less productive, being inferior . . . You name it!

When there is a promotion opportunity, single moms often are consciously or subconsciously excluded from the list of candidates, even though they are just as competent, with equal or better performance records. However, there are rarely any eyebrows raised. Few people would stand up for the well-qualified single moms, and most times not even those single moms stand up for themselves. Have you ever wondered why these very competent professional women often choose to accept these types of mistreatment at work? The reasons could be that some of these single moms are just too exhausted to take the efforts to stand up for themselves; some may have been defeated and wounded many times in the past and lost their hope for fair treatments; some are hindered by their unresolved guilt and shame associated with being a single mom; some may fear that they would lose the job and could not provide for their children; some lack a strong support system; and some lack resources and do not know what to do.

The truth is that single moms are often very loyal, committed, responsible, and accountable at home and at work. They might need to take a few more sick leaves to take care of their children. However, they often extend the same kind of care and dedication to their work. A little kind gesture from a coworker or boss will be returned with sincere appreciation and loyalty.

Do we single moms and professional women want to continue to be barred from advancement at our careers? Do we continue to allow ourselves to be stigmatized as poor performers at work? Are we still afraid to speak out and stand up for ourselves when we suffer mistreatment at work?

The answer is no. We want a change, and it is time for a change, not only for the benefit of single moms, but also for the benefit of our society. Out of frustration and repeated disappointment, we often can't even imagine there can be a change. But we can make a change, and we have to do it together!

Then the question is: What can we do to make a change in the existing environment? If we can, we should try to find a better job with a more supportive boss and coworkers. This complete transformation will give us a peaceful and positive working environment that is much needed. In order to do that, we need to be the experts in the field, through education and hard work. Unfortunately, often we are stuck in the current environment, and there seems no way out. In this situation, we can still make a change—we change ourselves. We can change our perceptions, beliefs, attitudes, and behaviors. We invest in ourselves and grow. Over time, we become the best, which might be enough evidence to change some coworkers' or bosses' misperceptions of single moms. If they refuse to see or accept the truth, then it's time to say goodbye to them, as we have become the experts in demand.

Have you been mistreated at work because of your single-mom status? How did that make you feel? How did you overcome it? #LunchNotes

(12) #JadedTruth

CYNDY FLEMMING, RN
NURSE & CLINICAL INSTRUCTOR

Defeat can become normal in the lives of some women. Single mothers are especially vulnerable to this possibility and are often too busy simply trying to survive to realize it has happened, even if they've subconsciously accepted it. This is the scary truth. We stay busy, telling ourselves we have to survive. We do not focus on correcting what seems to be the constant negativity surrounding us that we are disappointed in, and in time, we become jaded.

For those of us who left abusive marriages with our children, there is a certain voice within us questioning our decisions. Abuse is often tolerated because we fear raising children on one income, we fear forcing our children to explain why they do not have their other parent or must live between two homes, and we know that it will be hard on our own. Typically, it takes an extreme event for a woman to leave. By that time, the abuse has long become the norm, so that the mistreatment is subconsciously accepted in everyday life, spreading beyond the home and even to the workplace.

The day you leave, you are scared. You just faced a huge demon that most people would have never allowed in their lives but that you have chosen to live with for years. You are embarrassed, and you feel alone because you cannot talk about it without having to admit you allowed this to go on, when you do not even understand how it got to this point. This person constantly degraded you, telling you that you were not good enough and that you would never make it without them. Over time you believed them. They brought you down to fill themselves up. You did not realize it at the time, but you were dealing with an insecure person who saw more in you than you saw in yourself—which was a threat to them. You learned to keep yourself in the shadows. However, something happened to make you change the pattern you had accepted, to finally see that the mistreatment could no longer be tolerated. Then you wonder, were you right to leave? Can you even do this? Will your children have a better life or a worse one because of your decision? Or should you have stayed where you were mistreated—but at least your children could have both of their parents in the same home? If you say no, the jaded truth is for you.

Now that you have converted from an abused woman who always accepted inferiority and defeat to an empowered woman who is able to turn away from that situation onto anything better, you cannot go back. You have to work harder than ever before. You are now a single mom who is working full-time hours or more, and you must succeed to show your children that they deserve a better life, with a more positive environment surrounding them. No matter what, you cannot fail now. Family court will make you question everything, including your faith in the judicial system, which will not appear to protect your children. Lawyers and judges will ask if you truly believe it was the best choice to take your children out of a two-parent household to be in a single-parent home—with a parent who must work more hours to provide for them—and they will blatantly tell you that the abuse you endured and possible fear for your children is "water under the bridge" that cannot be considered a factor in their custodial decisions. You become mad. You are grinding every day on your own, without a support system, unable to tell people what is really going on in your life, and now a court will tear you down. This can lead anyone to become emotional. If you are not physically abused by your husband, you are still emotionally abused by him every day, and in the court room by additional people, demanding you state why you ruined your family's perfect world. Then you must go to work with this weight on your shoulders. You say everything is fine when anyone asks how you are. Remember why you left. You're not fine. You are tired, and you feel defeated over and over again, but your children deserve to be raised in an environment that respects you as a woman, and you deserve to show yourself the love of self-respect. You made the right decision. Be strong, and try your best to keep your emotions under control, or you will let the demon you left be right. That is not an option.

This is only one example of the unseen struggles women in the workforce face. If you have not gone through a similar case, imagine trying to go to work carrying this weight, unable to vent, no time for psychological counseling, aware that coworkers see you as a single mom who has other responsibilities, which will create barriers to career advancement or even expected productivity. No one can know or completely understand the struggles faced by single mothers who left abusive relationships. There is a stigma that accompanies the title of a single mother, when it should be viewed as a strength. Women who have endured this—yet still show up every day, taking on additional college courses to improve themselves and their whole family's success, while balancing a broken home life that is healing in transition and setting aside their own immediate gratification—demonstrate great resilience, power, and loyalty. That is a rare find in today's workforce. These are the women who, in making those same choices that created the single mother some employers look down on, have made the right decisions to better their lives. They prioritize responsibilities while silently suffering yet remain focused on what is important.

These women must keep a steady income flowing into the homes they are head of. This can lead to accepting more mistreatment, now in the workforce, which is not justified but tolerated because you cannot go back. This is the jaded truth. You must grind and keep pushing yourself to persevere, because you left for a reason. You will accept mistreatment in the workforce, sadly at times from other women even, because you have to do what is best for your children. You are a strong woman who cannot go back. You must work. Use your defeat to fuel your drive. Now work harder. There is no time to feel defeated but time to learn and empower yourself. You will never be perfect. There is no perfect family. You have more to prove in every aspect of your life now. It is enough to make anyone jaded, and it is the truth you live. When mistreatment happens, you must learn to be smarter about how you react to it in order to succeed. I use my anger and frustration to fuel me to do better. Sometimes emotions can interfere with how well you handle being mistreated at work. I try to stay focused on improving outcomes, and that includes being a positive female role model to my children and teaching the importance of self-respect and love in hopes that my children have a better future, with much better decisions made. One day I will be able to forgive and let go of the injustices that created this jaded truth. For now, I celebrate the small victories and keep grinding and hope that there are other women out there who are willing to come forward to empower one another rather than compound negativity.

Lunch Notes

What is your jaded truth? #LunchNotes

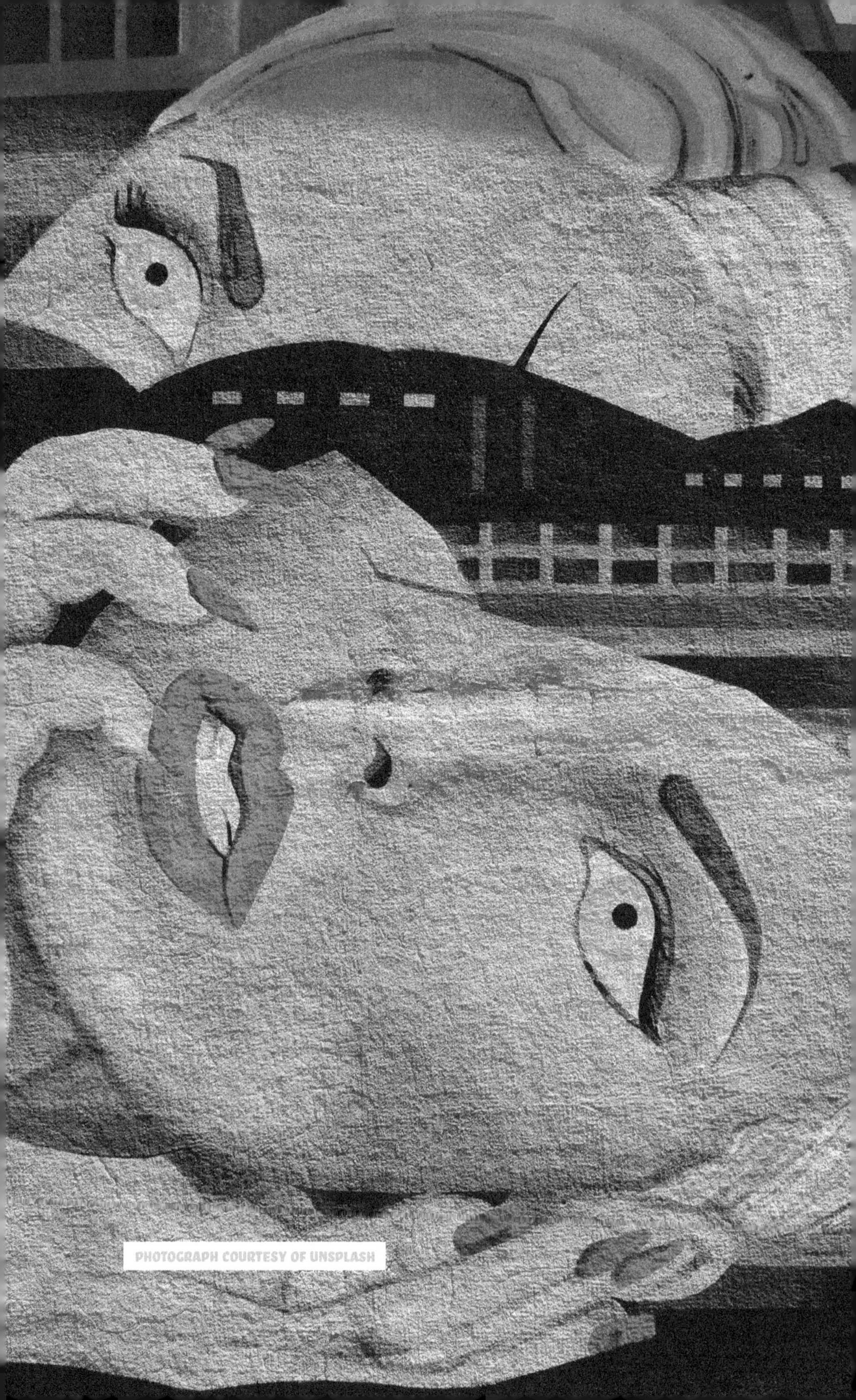

PHOTOGRAPH COURTESY OF UNSPLASH

(13) #MoreThanAPrettyFace

MEGAN COREY
CERTIFIED HEALTH COACH & WELLNESS EXPERT

Women are making leaps and bounds in the workforce, so why are we still stereotyping about someone's worth by the way they look or their age? We've all done it: "OMG, look at that girl. She's beautiful and super cool, but what the hell does she know about this?" Don't judge a book by its cover. Just because someone looks a certain way doesn't mean they don't have the smarts and motivation to kick ass. Think about it—have you ever been in a situation where you've been treated differently just because of how you looked, before you were even given the opportunity to show your worth? Whether it's age, race, or gender discrimination, each of us has gone through this at some point in our lives. I can't say this is getting any better in the world we live in today, but I can say there are things we can do about it to help influence the change for the better.

I've been in plenty of situations where I have gotten a glance and then was passed over to see what the gentleman next to me had to say. Or I was met with, "What does she know? She's just pretty," before even being given the opportunity to show my capabilities. But I didn't let that stop me. I ignored and pushed on, continuing to do my work and giving it all I had. I established a good name for myself by the products I was submitting, the respect I was giving and receiving, and the leadership and mentoring I was providing; I had developed credibility and my "worth." You have to put the people who are out to get you out of your head and show what you can do, because in their eyes actions speak louder than words. They want proof that you are capable and important enough to keep around. That you are intelligent and provide meaningful input in different situations. There isn't anything you should change about yourself for anyone else—keep being you, and all the beauty that you are, and your walk, will do the talking.

Women are now getting more attention than men because of the movements pushing us forward, so we need to take that momentum and move with it. Don't let someone boss you around or tell you what you're worth. The whole "you" is who you are and what you have to give, so give it, and give it with poise and positivity. Once you start seeing your worth and accepting and receiving your accomplishments with an open heart, it will only make you want to strive to push further and be better than you are today. Pause, take that deep breath, and keep that head high to achieve your dreams and goals.

Have you ever felt that your looks were the only thing people could focus on while doubting your credibility? #LunchNotes

(14) #ForBetterOrForWorse

KATIE LEUNG
TEACHER

A war surrounds me. My world has completely collapsed within itself, and I'm left alone to deal with it. I'm in a dark space. The cold is piercing my bones and freezing the rest of my body from the inside out. My heart beats faintly to fight it; whatever hope I have left remains in the feeble rhythm of what I think must have been my soul. The explosions outside accentuate every fifth beat, creating an awkward, irritating tempo around my head and behind my ears. How is it that I can hear my heart beating over the explosions? And that I can hear men screaming and children crying? Are they my children? Is that man someone I used to know? I haven't seen my husband in almost four years. The thought makes my mouth dry and the acid rise up in my chest. The tears are there, and it takes all of me to fight them off. Because I have cried alone for so long, to cry for others as well is shifting the pace and pattern of my already weak heart. And my heart is all I have left.

There is still a faint smell of gasoline from bombs going off, and I wonder if there will be more. I can't predict them these days. It used to be that I could feel a blast coming: the earth would quiver beneath me, and the vibrations would tingle throughout my head and chest. I used to be able to coach myself through the loudness, the realness of war. I would be able to anticipate the ugliness; I'd allow myself anxious, terrified tears, the embarrassment of not inhaling enough air to even let out a dignified cry, and I'd struggle through as one bomb after another would collide with concrete, sending black smoke into the already polluted, silent air. That was what I was *supposed* to do. I knew it would change the mindset of my life—accepting the things I could not change, even though I had already tried to change the things I could not accept. I knew those crucial moments would make or break me, and more often than not, after wrestling with hopelessness and guilt, I decided to stay broken. Now, when the familiar ticking goes off, when I hear the guns cock, I feel a slight ache in my chest, a pull to ready myself. Then, I choose numbness. I don't even prepare for the sounds because, foolishly, I think it makes me stronger. It's just as difficult to react as it is to prepare, so why bother? I watch the rubble around me crumble to dust, and I'm sad that I can't even feel sad anymore. The tears are still there, but at least I am no longer hyperventilating with anxiety. It's eerily peaceful, and I can feel my children watching.

The tiny dwellings deteriorate haphazardly every day. Through the kaleidoscope of my mind, I see broken glass where windows used to be, where light used to shine and bend and seek brilliant colors when the sun chose to visit. The black mouths of them silently cry out for repair, thirsty for light to reach through and warm the people who may or may not build lives there again, in case the sun does return. There are few foundations left; a decade of sheltering and nurturing human lives seems pointless now that my world has fallen apart, all the while shaking its judgmental, pointed finger at me for not living up to expectations. Twisted steel rods cowardly poke out from their concrete stumps, longing to be straightened.

There is a man's face I see in my dreams, when I can finally sleep at night. I have a blanket that doesn't cover me enough, and I wake up to a cold sweat on my chest. Sometimes, I wake up wishing I had fought him off, angrily reliving the times I felt neglected and used. But many times, I wake up wishing he had come to apologize, stroke my hair, and tell me that all the success and glory in the world wasn't as important as me. It would have been pure and true, white with light and hope for a future that, in this life, would never again be possible. I'd ache for that kind of love, for it meant I was still alive somewhere, that I could recognize vivid colors, taste spicy food, sing in the shower, and appreciate better things after enduring the worst. My perception changes to varying shades of gray as I struggle to appreciate all of my subdued colors.

War isn't appreciative. It's selfish and full of its own insecurities, kept alive by hateful words, excessive weapons, and disproportionate pride. I've tried to be the bigger person in this inadequate life dedicated to measuring egos. I've accepted my rations, my station, with humility and the notion that I must accept values I don't remember agreeing to. I've listened to the propaganda, and I've pretended for the sake of peace. I've been chastised for being ungrateful—the words coming from my own mouth: "You're taken care of, aren't you? At least you are alive. God bless every day that you wake up, for it is another gift." It doesn't matter that I don't believe in God.

My knees crack as I crawl around the space that used to be my walk-in closet. Years ago, my husband and I joked about how big it was in here. Oh, to be able to joke about privilege! Now it's just dirt, mud, and stones smashed together—in a way that a toddler would be proud of—into a makeshift shelter that is a haven for dust. Honestly, I could have survived with only him in there. I didn't need what was outside of that—an entire house or life in the suburbs—to feel happy. A year ago, I knotted together remnants of colorful silk scarves and ties to make a curtain—to hide what, I'm not sure—a life that used to be and now isn't?

I pull the pieces of fabric away, and a long sliver of dim light hits the floor. It immediately reminds me of the times he and I would sneak in here while the children played. I was so sure he loved me then. I'd lie on the scratchy carpet and stare at his tailored suits fraternizing with each other as they stood erect, and near the top, their little pocket squares arrogantly peeked out of their high-rise compartments. I think that's how he coped with the war. Maybe I helped him feel alive; maybe our secret moments helped him to feel in control during all of the fighting—like a soldier going into battle who indulges in one last rendezvous. I shake my head at how that used to seem romantic to me.

The soldiers have their regimens. The soldiers—men and women—follow their orders. They see people as pawns, strategic pieces to move out of sight, out of mind, not realizing they are puppets in this show as well, with strings attached to every move. I wonder if they realize that the example they're setting is fake, that they make the rest of us gag when we smell them coming, like when they used to stomp their filthy boots upon the rug in my foyer while I raced to salute them in ridiculous high heels. I realized then, in my folded toes and awkward ankles, hobbling against a tight mermaid-shaped dress, that these soldiers were brainwashed, and if they were to be considered examples of real, live human beings, I'd much rather die in my closet hole than pretend I belonged anywhere safe.

I wonder if they remember me. I used to paint my face and twist my highlighted hair neat and flush against my scalp, a vision of the acceptable daily uniform. Hell, I even tried baking to get along with the rest of the domestic goddesses. I'd tell jokes and share bottles of wine and remind my comrades of what it was like to speak openly, to enjoy our own simple company. Every once in a while, I'd hear their truth come out, and I welcomed the words, warm with loving intention in a moment shared with trust. I'd feel a pull and a connection as we discussed ways in which the war was supposed to be chivalrous, when really it was just an exercise to help our men assert power and feel significant. But just as quickly as those connections were made, they would disappear into a world of guilt, where Big Brother reminded us that women have made it so far, and we have so much to be thankful for. I was polite and didn't offend anyone. I was careful to become a delightful source of small talk. I was organized and timely, but never quite obedient enough. It was charming at first, until they realized I wasn't joking.

He, on the other hand, became a general. He was chosen to lead the charge into a more "lucrative" life, and so he commanded the field from the comfort of his leather recliner. I hear he was brilliant. He saved lives and let others go in the most respectable way possible—all for the cause of continuing to stay alive, to exist, to extend all of humanity's "quality of life," as he would say. He called the right plays and fell in love with ambition. But I didn't want to merely fight alongside him and other men. I didn't want to feel guilty for speaking up for what I wanted as my own quality of life. Ambition could never compare to love, and love was worth fighting for. I wanted to fight for my mother, my sister, my daughter. I wanted a revolution.

Part of me still feels like I'm sixteen. I'm alone and unsure, full of angst, and vulnerable to every person's judgment and whispered comments. I'm rebellious because deep down, I know what's being fed to me doesn't feel right, and why should I feel badly about the essence of me? This hurt, this hopeless disappointment is a result of smaller, loveless transactions, deals made for power, and status that grew into a life I don't recognize anymore.

The man I dream about is my ex-husband. The war we survived is an emotional war I still try to quell, although putting ink to paper doesn't make a peace treaty. I am still my sixteen-year-old self, paralyzed in a closet, trying to decide between an outfit that feels comfortable or one that risks judgment. I feel much closer to that teenager, filled with life and daring, than the woman I've become twenty years later, divorced and alone. But I convince her every day that it is better to fight alone forever than it is to stay married and lonely, regardless of judgment.

And in that closet, behind a discarded, careless pile of wood, glass shards, and debris, I spot some fabric from an old dress I only wore once, to one of his holiday parties. When I unfold it, shiny sequins jiggle excitedly, winking at me as if we share an ancient secret. The dress is gone, but this one tiny piece, hand sewn with shiny promises across the top, is just long enough to add to the curtain I pulled off earlier. I tie it to the very middle of the curtain rod, making sure the sequins face out. I want the sun to find me and reflect what little light is left in this hole. I beg it to find this small, but significant, piece of my past—a dress I bought on clearance in order to look expensive for people I would never want to invite into my home anyway. In my mind, I see the hot light refract and split and find new dwellings to warm. I see hardened women's faces, flushed with sweat, peering out of camps, and I hear their children singing softly, but confident in their harmonies. I see soldiers walking backward into the shadows.

In what way does a physical war resemble an emotional one? Is one more traumatic than the other? #LunchNotes

The narrator mentions her mermaid dress and heels, slicked-back hair, and painted face. What role do you think she's portraying? Why was she so conscious of this goal? #LunchNotes

In what ways do light and colored fabric represent hope or love in this piece? #LunchNotes

In the end, you get a sense the soldiers are marching back into the shadows. What does this mean for the narrator? #LunchNotes

(15) #WhitePicketFence

ALEX & BELL
RESEARCHER & WRITER AT WANDERLUST MARRIAGE
HTTPS://WANDERLUSTMARRIAGE.COM/

Go to school, get a job, get married, buy a house, and have a family. This is the formula for the perfect life wrapped in a white picket fence, or so we're told at least. There is no alternative formula taught to us from a young age for living a successful life. But what happens if you don't want to follow this formula, or what if you can't, or what if it's even a bit of both?

We got off to the "right start" by going to college—tick! Got jobs and got married to each other—tick, tick. We were nailing this successful-life thing on paper, and all by our midtwenties.

We'd met in a hostel while backpacking in Europe. And as the story goes, we were literally thrust into the same bed by fate, Alex on the top bunk and Bell on the bottom. What were we doing in suburbia now, already sunk in the daily grind? Life wasn't bad, but you get one shot at life, and we decided to go off script.

We packed up a modest and comfortable life to move to the Netherlands, close to where we initially met. From the world that tells us we need to follow the formula, we heard that we were brave and adventurous. But neither of us would use those words to describe what we did; we just got organized and moved our stuff.

Were the three and a half years we spent living in Amsterdam all windmills, cheese, and tulips? No. No sugarcoating—we arrived in 2008, at the beginning of the financial crisis. We always had enough, so our bills were paid, but making an unexpected twenty-euro purchase was a big deal. The historic center of Amsterdam, filled with canals and seventeenth-century buildings, remains the most beautiful place we have called home. We had friends and potluck meals and picnics on the canals. We found alternative ways to stretch what we had by couch surfing and making new connections when we traveled. Is Dutch society better than US society? Not really. At times we were very forthrightly told things like we'd "taken a house off the rental market for a Dutch person." There are assholes everywhere.

After three and a half years in Amsterdam, it was time for us to find a new home. Deciding where to go next was a back-and-forth dance that we tangoed. Deciding where to call home is no easy task. But the cards lined up to call Dublin, Ireland, home for over two years.

Quickly enough, we settled into our apartment as well as our new lives. Living in Amsterdam, we'd picked up tricks for finding friends, and the expat community is typically an open and welcoming place. The problem is the transient nature of expats, but the wonderful thing about such a community is that it is quick to welcome people. The shared experience of being alone in a country far from where you call home creates a quick intimacy that can take years to cultivate with people in your home country. The hard part is saying many goodbyes as people move on.

The amazing iridescent green of Ireland comes at a cost; many days are gray and rainy, and this can drag on for weeks. Not everyone needs a lot of sunshine to thrive, but for Alex the long cloudy stretches began to weigh heavily. For two consecutive summers, Alex's then eighty-five-year-old father came to visit. We noticed a significant decrease in his ability to get around on the second visit, a sign that his good years were fading. Alex couldn't help but feel he wanted to be closer to his childhood home than a transatlantic flight—especially since his father had repeatedly made the long flight for visits.

As a new opportunity for Bell presented itself across the Atlantic, which would put us just a short domestic flight away from Alex's father, we felt conflicted. We had sought change from the United States, and Alex had begun to rebuild a career around that change with a website focusing on travel and expat life. For Bell, the novelty of being a foreigner would remain, but for Alex that would change.

We took the plunge and returned to the United States. There were days when Alex felt like a stranger in his own country, and this feeling was unsettling. Bell felt overwhelmed doing the grocery shopping in large and overly bright stores where the choices appeared limitless.

After living in Europe for six years, we found that Boston felt familiar with its European-style architecture, yet foreign with the multitude of chain restaurants on each corner. The size of Boston is much larger than Amsterdam or Dublin. Some family relationships had already been strained by the time abroad, but others were happy to see us return. But for Alex, the gesture of his sacrifice did not feel appreciated.

Coming back has meant sometimes being grilled on what our ultimate plans are. Surely it was time to get back on track; after all, we were no longer in our twenties. "Are you going to buy a house, and what about a family?" We still hear this from both friends and family, even though it has now been five years since we returned.

Eventually, we did meet with realtors and have attempted to start a family. But both boxes remain unticked. Many believe, with valid points, that children are the meaning of life. After all, if everyone stopped having children, society as we know it would collapse. But what if you tried for years and cannot have kids? What's the meaning of life then? After years living abroad, perhaps we're still searching for that answer for ourselves. At this moment, we can't tell you if we'll tick off either of these boxes, but we doubt we'll do it in any traditional way. And there will never be a white picket fence holding us back.

What is your alternative "white picket fence"? #LunchNotes

(16) #ForeverStrong

KELLY SCOTT
OWNER OF FOREVER STRONG FITNESS

I don't have a story about being equally qualified as a man, yet not being given the same opportunities. My story is about someone who had every disadvantage, lack of qualifications, lack of education, and lack of resources, who just relied on grit and determination to crawl out of a pit she was raised to think it was her duty to stay in.

In 2008, I left my husband, my job, and a controlling religious group. My family and friends abandoned me. I had no idea what would happen next, but I knew I couldn't stand one more day living a shackled existence. I wanted more from life. . . . More positivity. More enjoyment. More accomplishment. More confidence. More experiences. More strength. More energy. More fun. More passion. More fulfillment. More friendships and better relationships. More purpose—a greater purpose. More challenges. More opportunities. More doing. More action. More success.

At the same time, I needed less. . . . Less inhibition. Less fear. Less drama. Less toxicity. Less negativity. Less agitation. Less depression. Less barriers. Less struggle. Less dead ends. Less procrastinating. Less self-deprecation. Less stress. Less boredom. Less failure.

Living in a high-control religious sect means doing what you're told. I received harsh treatment when I doubted anything. No talking back, no independent thought, and no "normal" fun was allowed. I couldn't even attempt to pursue friends or activities outside the group. During my time in "God's organization," I was raped, violated of my dignity, stolen from, abused, misled, blackmailed, forced to work without pay, and bullied. Because I had no formal education past the seventh grade, I didn't think I'd achieve anything good or worth having. I lived a sheltered life and trembled in fear of what the "evil world" would do to me.

I spent decades enduring my life instead of enjoying it.

I had enough. I decided it would be better to live one day in freedom and peace than an eternity in oppression. Determined to find serenity, I left everything behind.

I believed I'd lose the protection of God, and I expected the "Devil's evil world" to attack me. It was a risk I was willing to take.

I used to believe the purpose of life was to endure misery on earth until you go to heaven. Now, I believe the purpose of life is simply to enjoy each day.

It wasn't easy. At first, I was barely getting by. I had to shift from tolerating a mediocre life to building a purposeful one. It meant starting out homeless, with no family and no friends. I struggled with two jobs, as a bartender and a personal trainer.

I had no money, credit, connections, home, education, family, or close friends. I lived out of my car. My name was still on the mortgage my ex-husband hadn't paid in eighteen months. My credit was shot; a business loan wasn't an option.

I had to learn how to survive. Quickly.

My first few weeks out, I expected every day to be my last, so I became a daredevil, nearly taunting Satan to attack me by engaging in risky behavior.

My Mountain of Disadvantages:

In the few short years from when I left my husband until I started my business, I faced challenges in gaining employment and starting a business. The only way for me to overcome these obstacles was to view each as an opportunity to conquer a challenge, not a roadblock to achieving potential.

Here are some of the disadvantages I faced externally:

- Sheltered upbringing: homeschooled on and off with extreme restrictions on music, reading material, entertainment, and interactions with non-Jehovah's Witnesses
- Married young
- Messy divorce

- Recovery from a hostile marriage in which I was a domestic slave and ownership of my body was given to my husband
- Prevented from getting an education: ripped out of school
- All secular education discouraged by parents and religious authority figures
- No college education
- Extreme avoidance of self-help books, philosophy, and intellectual pursuits of the world
- Lack of knowledge and access to private and public resources for assistance
- Did not fit into a "category" for assistance from public agencies (no children, not a minority)
- Elders (authority figures) determined to keep me in my place
- Restricted from developing critical-thinking skills
- Financial insolvency—no money, no savings, no assets
- No support from family—rejected by closest family members
- No relationship with extended family members
- Loss of every adult and childhood friendship (why I had no "worldly" friendships)
- Grieving the loss of both parents and a sister
- Terrible credit: short sale and late car payments
- Bad decision not to use a lawyer: signed a property settlement agreement that was unenforceable
- Loss of steady employment: no ties to former coworkers
- No teachers or mentors
- Homelessness, then unstable housing, then shared housing (basement dwelling)
- Lack of household possessions (living basics like a mattress and furniture)
- Loss of most sentimental objects (photos, jewelry, gifts)
- Loss of entire emotional support system: church, family, friends
- Being an outcast
- No personal "connections": no college buddies, no friends from middle school or high school, no drinking buddies, no sports teams, no teams, no groups, no personal friends from prior

employment, no girls from the office, no book club, no clubs, no church groups, no political-party affiliations, no hobby groups, no ladies' nights, no family traditions, no gym buddies, no fan clubs, no ethnic or cultural groups (we were taught to keep separate from the world)

- No institutions to turn to: no affiliations to any groups, no clubs, no schools, churches

Internal Disadvantages:

- My limiting belief that women were subservient to men: men were created to lead, and women were made for support roles
- The limiting belief that doubting the "truth" was a sin
- Achievement discouraged: limiting belief that achievement is haughtiness and pride is against God
- Living with the emotional burden of displeasing God, family, authority figures
- My limiting belief that ambition was selfish
- My limiting beliefs about money: pursuing financial security was equal to materialism, and rich people were enemies of God

Not Defined by My Disadvantages

Accepting my disadvantages did not mean I let them define me. Well, nobody's perfect, and sometimes I still succumb to self-pity. For the most part, however, I had to ditch the poor-me victim mentality in order to move forward.

- Just because I did not have a formal education didn't mean I was uneducated. Hell, I spent more time studying and developing myself by the age of twenty-five than most people do in their whole lives. I just had to learn how to transition those skills from being an evangelist for Jehovah to being an evangelist for me and those who work with me.

- Just because my family disconnected from me does not mean I was unloved, rejected. I had to find the love inside myself first and earn my self-worth one personal victory at a time.
- Just because I left the faith does not mean I was wicked, immoral, or deserving of punishment. I was an honest, loving, and upright citizen.
- Even though much of what I thought I knew about God, my purpose, and spirituality turned out to be a lie, I was not a liar or a fool. I was a person who lacked critical-thinking skills, and those skills can be learned.

I'm not going to run down the entire list of disadvantages, but you get the point. Whatever your disadvantage or disability is, you have the right to choose how to define yourself.

I avoided feelings of rejection and failure by choosing alternative routes on my path. If the path forward was blocked, I went around. Don't think of it as a detour; think of it as taking the scenic route.

Focused on What I Did Have

Despite being the underdog, I did have a few advantages: my desire to thrive, my determination to succeed, and my commitment to my health. I hate to see people squander their health. If you are in good health, please don't waste the *one* resource with unlimited potential, a resource nearly 100 percent in your control.

From that platform, I left my hostile marriage, abandoned my religion, quit my unfulfilling job, and restarted my career and my life as a personal trainer. I closed the door on my former life and wasn't looking back. I chose personal training as my passion because it fulfilled my desire to really make a difference in people's lives.

And in just a few short weeks with my clients, I was really making a difference in their health and their lives. Over the years, some have even thanked me for actually saving their lives and their health. I loved that feeling and still do. That feeling of making a difference, a personal reward in my employment, fed my desire to press on.

Fast-forward tenish years, and I have a thriving personal-training business with a team of people who support my vision.

I wrote this story to inspire the women who hold themselves back when circumstances are less than ideal. I hope that my story will encourage you to keep moving forward and never compare yourself to others who you think have perceived advantages over you.

If it was easy, everyone would be at the top. If you want more from your life, you have to go out and grab it by any means necessary. You may have some bad experiences along the way, and you'll probably end up with an awesome story to tell. Open your mind to pursue experiences for the sake of those experiences. You'll have some great experiences that way, and you'll learn more from the bad experiences than the good ones. Even if you keep your story to yourself, you will find the conqueror that lies within you.

I bet you are facing serious problems right now. I challenge you to grow bigger than your problems. If I became #ForeverStrong, you can too!

Share your story about when you were in a disadvantaged situation but did not let that stop you. #LunchNotes

(17) #AcademicTestsAreNotYourWorth

J.F HEART
LICENSED CLINICAL PSYCHOTHERAPIST

FAILED. The aggressive, bold, large red word. The word that held me hostage. Captive in my own heart, mind, body, and soul. My dreams were shattered in an instant by the computer screen. I was trapped by my professional board's standards and the archaic idea that test scores are the only way this aspiring woman could be given my supposedly earned rite of passage and be permitted to practice my passion—the passion of helping others find their truth, cultivate their dreams, and nurture their growth.

The deep hue of the color red, the one-syllable word, the symbolism of the testing center equaling my own personal and literal hell. Don't breathe too loud. No eating. Don't stretch your arms. I must go to the bathroom within ten minutes.

When I returned to my cell, my glasses were inspected, the fingerprints of the proctors blurring the vision I had created for myself. My hair clip was taken away from me, allowing the sweat I feared to trickle down my face and drip onto the keyboard, slowly washing away my sense of self.

My jaw was so tight I could actually feel the black and blue marks rising to the surface as I attempted to answer the purposely crafted, mind-crushing multiple-choice questions that made no sense in real life and had no application to my clinical work. Fighting the natural urge to answer what was in the best interest of the patient, I thought like the test, regardless of what my intuition and numerous years of hands-on experience told me. "Become the test," I said to myself.

The smell in the room was always the same and acutely recognizable. This was the third time I had attempted to pass this exam. My body chemistry changed in the parking lot. Hell, let's be honest, I couldn't even feel my body at this point. I dismissed the countless hours of grounding and mindfulness coping tools I had learned and the cognitive behavioral therapy techniques I believed I had rehearsed. The hundreds of thousands of hours and monetary compensation I had sacrificed all came down to this.

All that separated me from claiming myself and the well-earned, meaningless letters after my last name was the construct of PASS/FAIL. The thirty-four years of experience I had collected, lived for, studied for, chased after, they did not matter. I was not human, rather a number, and my life, in this moment, was once again paused.

I was forced to submit, repress, and swallow the passion that ignited my very being. Held by the ethics of the employers I worked for, frequently not in the best interest of the patient. Expected to show up to work the next day, smiling like a cheerleader and holding a mental and physical space for those who were in trauma. Screw my own trauma. It did not matter, as I had not earned the credentials.

PASSED. After a year and a half of questioning, doubting, and hating myself, I finally did it! By my professional board's standards, I was now allowed to set up the private practice I had always longed for. I no longer had to cater the type of care I offered, my treatment plans, or the patient's outcome to a system that had never laid eyes on the patient. I could finally be the tool in the treatment room to transform kindness, empathy, and change. I could be with the patient, in all their glory, and design the sessions I delivered based on their needs and wants.

Unfortunately, this was my story. Fortunately for you, however, it does not have to be yours. Sure, pending your path in life, you may have to take licensing exams. There may ultimately be a governing body that may or may not dictate your professional path. Do not, on behalf of those who came before you, define yourself based on the shallow, completely unrelatable, and nonliving numeric system.

You have a choice; we all do. Choose to support, seek, and empower one another. Find the strength to intentionally surround yourself with people who believe in and genuinely see you. If your warrior sisters and brothers do not immediately offer themselves and are not able to reveal their vulnerability, keep going. Find your pack. You are worth it; your story does matter. You touch many lives, even when you do not feel that others recognize you.

When you feel alone, dig deep, for I promise you that others too feel this way. Your life is a beautiful mosaic that ultimately can be used to transform anything and anyone. You do not have to live in the world those before you created, not in the context of your self-worth. Hone in on your unique and magical gifts, spreading the seeds of the fierce possibility of freedom and allowing your pain to be transformed through the legacy of embracing and being real with others.

Lunch Notes

Share a story when you overcame adversity. #LunchNotes

(18) #IDontBite

GRACE KEENAN, JD
LAWYER

My colleague disclosed to me that he never eats alone with a woman other than his wife. The composed superego side of my brain responded to this statement by thinking, "Honorable intentions aside, such a rule only serves to reinforce the glass ceiling." My less refined id flashed, "Screw you, I don't bite."

"I don't bite" is now my internal motto whenever a work opportunity is jeopardized by my female form. When I joined the workforce, I thought I was prepared for anything. My mental checklist looked as follows:

- Smart and motivated—check
- Groomed in a pleasing, not "going to a nightclub," way—check
- Thin but not too thin—check
- Attractive but not too attractive—check
- Good sense of humor—check
- Not overly sensitive—check
- No children—check

But the above won't get you a business lunch with a male colleague who fears that a moment alone with a female-not-his-wife will lead to a moment of regret. Because that is what "I don't dine alone without women other than my wife" means. It means either that the man has no self-control and views women as nothing but temptresses, or that the man believes women cannot be trusted and are sure to turn a routine business lunch into the next episode of *Real Housewives*.

And, frighteningly, you never know where men with such beliefs are lurking. You may steadily advance for years only to suddenly have your dream position foreclosed by a man intimidated by your cursed female form. However, short of major surgery, there are steps that both men and women can take to help remove such barriers (this is not an exhaustive list):

- Disregard certain life "rules" when at work. It may be perfectly reasonable for you to not have one-on-one meetings with the opposite sex during your leisure time, but work is different. If the new intern could use some advice and no one else feels like sushi, go anyway. Business lunches are often essential to advancement, and no one should be robbed of such opportunities simply because they are in the wrong packaging.
- Wives and girlfriends, encourage your partners to treat female colleagues the same as they treat their male colleagues. Marriage and fidelity are sacred, but the cute female intern shouldn't suffer because you're insecure. If your marriage is that fragile, go to counseling. But don't ruin someone's career.
- We are inundated with sexual harassment trainings, but such trainings do nothing to remedy the boys' club atmosphere facilitated by the rule to never eat alone with a woman other than the wife. Supervisors should be trained on methods that ensure equal opportunities amongst staff and should be encouraged to mentor associates regardless of sex. By making one-on-one meetings a part of a company's advancement framework, such meetings are normalized and are less likely to raise an eyebrow.

Finally, if all else fails, remind the offender, ever so gently, that you don't bite.

What suggestions would you add to the above list? #LunchNotes

What was your mental checklist when you prepared for your first professional job? #LunchNotes

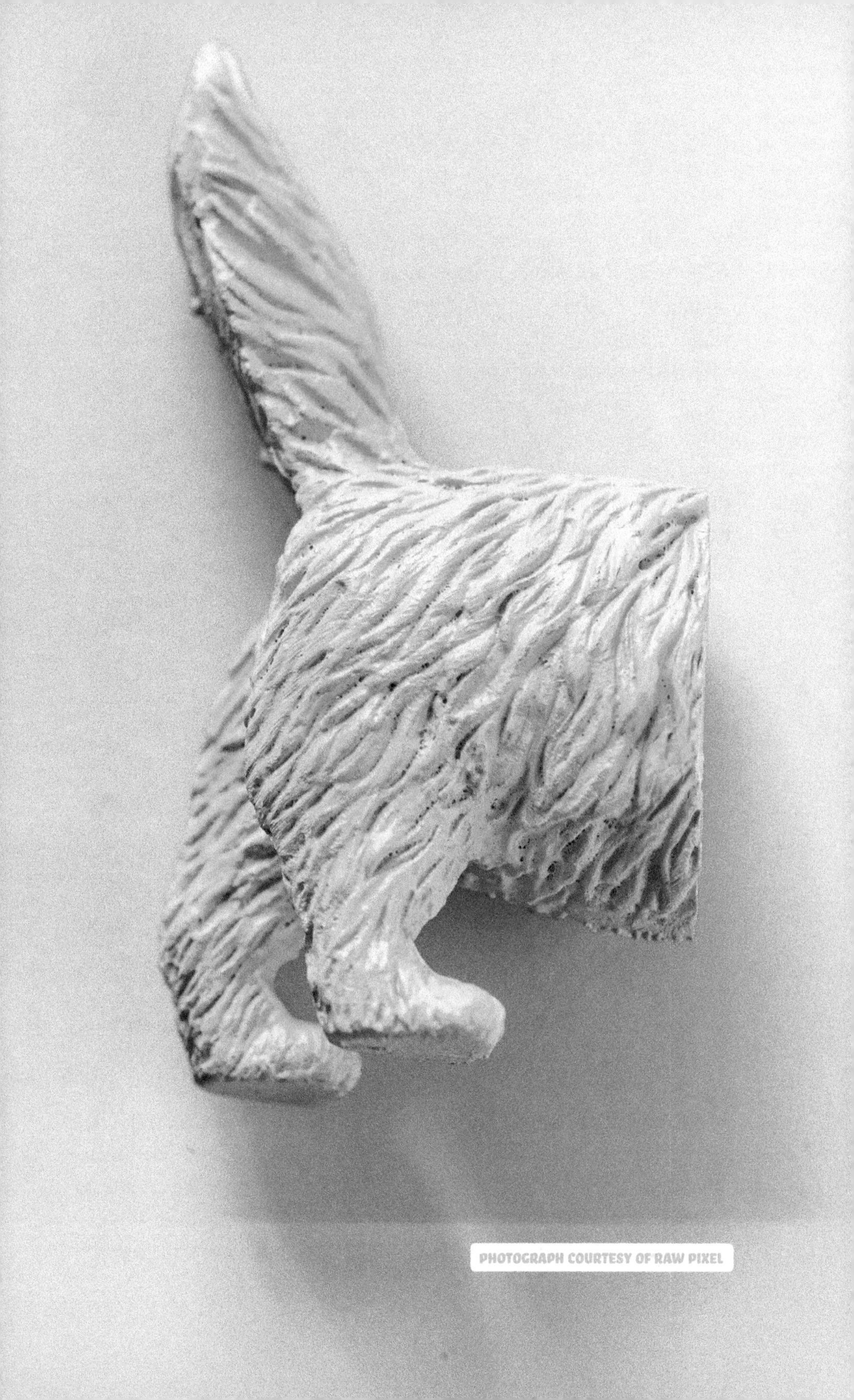

PHOTOGRAPH COURTESY OF RAW PIXEL

(19) #Brownnosers

We are all too familiar, unfortunately, with those who have a knack for sniffing out the bottoms of superiors. They have the uncanny talent of finding the butthole within the first few hours of landing and knowing which butthole has the greatest elasticity that will accept their body's insertion into the warm cavity.

The interesting thing about the brownnoser is their ability to not hate themselves before, during, and after the cavity insertion. They have trained their gag reflex to accept this daily process as easily as drinking their morning coffee. And we need to remember that brownnosing is not a one-time event but requires a daily consistency.

Typically, brownnosers recognize that they have very little innate talent and competency and rely on this generations-old technique in order to advance in their career. I was once told to watch out for those people who have not produced much in their careers but are in high leadership positions, as they reached those positions not because of creativity, talent, or hard work, but rather through the daily insertion into warm body cavities. These people tend to be highly insecure and will try to derail those around them whom they view as competent and talented (see "#Threat" for additional detail).

Characteristically, there is only one butthole in a workplace that has enough elasticity to be willing to accept the insertion process. If there is more than one brownnoser, this becomes a race for the daily insertion, and jealousy and competition can arise because there is not enough space in such a confined cavity for more than one body.

I will have to admit that as a young woman, I saw those around me advance at a rapid pace through this brownnosing technique. So, I tried it. As soon I felt my lips graze the hypothetical baby-smooth skin of the superior's bottom, my gag reflex acted up. I massaged my acupressure point for nausea and vomiting, held my breath, and continued the dive into the dark cavity. I can never forget that experience. It was horrible. The stink of that day follows me to this day whenever I think about that experience. I immediately started pacing and rocking myself.

I hated myself. I was disgusted with myself. And I knew my parents had not spent decades of *their* lives making sure that I was groomed to be an independent, secure person only to see me flounder with feces. I decided that this need to train my gag reflex and suppress the self-hate was not worth it and that I would continue my career liking who I was and being proud of my accomplishments.

Have you witnessed brownnosing in your workplace? Try writing about your experiences with a comedic twist. #LunchNotes

(20) #WorkHarder

Advice from women on the trodden path before me: "You just have to work harder." However, when does working harder translate into an outcome beyond the vicious cycle?

The glass ceiling is a barrier reinforced through manipulation tactics, denial of opportunities, and moving the goalpost, all to create confusion and a barrier to success. It is possible that your goalpost isn't even on the playing field but is sitting on the factory floor, disassembled. So, it doesn't matter how many checked boxes you hit on the playing field—you will never reach that goalpost.

Thus, when do our hammer-like tools of degrees, training, and hard work stop rebounding off the acrylic-glass ceiling?

When has working harder translated or not translated into the desired outcome? #LunchNotes

(21) #Inconvenience

I grew up during a time when girls were taught that they could grow up to be whatever they wanted to be.

I believed foolishly as a child that the fight for equality was over, due to the hard work done by generations before us. *Empowerment* was the word of my generation, with more and more women getting higher degrees and engaging in male-dominated fields.

Imagine my surprise when I realized that I was empowered only until the time of inconvenience. Once I started asserting myself in an area that others were not comfortable with, my empowerment was no longer a plus but rather a negative. Once my views started infringing upon convenience, where the other person would have to adjust to my needs, then the glass ceiling would appear with bonded materials. Empowerment doesn't have to die once the inconvenience boundary is breached or becomes uncomfortable. This is when it really matters.

When did your empowerment cause inconvenience, and how did you navigate past the boundary? #LunchNotes

PHOTOGRAPH COURTESY OF UNSPLASH

(22) #Threat

Let's stop for a moment to delve deep into how you are feeling and see if any of the glass analogies (tempered-glass ceiling, acrylic-glass layer, glass slipper) have hit a nerve. Can you relate? I'm going to let you in on a little secret: very likely it is not you, and it is them.

It really is not you, and it is them. You are a threat to their ideology.

Bully behavior is often not well understood in the workplace and not talked about. There is limited awareness of this very effective manipulation and control technique. Bully behavior in the workplace is common and stems from insecurities. On-the-job harassment is an effective way to prevent threats from stepping out of their predefined roles

Star performers, or those who step out of their stereotypes, create a threat to a bully's insecurities. This threat is handled with extremely effective bully techniques, or on-the-job harassment, which can include aggression, hostility, being overly critical or condescending, gossip spreading, and character assassination behaviors.

Avoiding bullies is incredibly hard because they have adapted to hiding and refining their behaviors, so these behaviors are not so apparent. These confusing behaviors may put you, the victim, in constant paralysis. The bullies may see you as a threat to their ideology or ego, or they hold this fear that you will outshine them, steal their jobs, infringe upon their entitlement and privilege—whatever the threat may be. The typical response to such a threat is to start bully behavior immediately, which can include tactics to intimidate you, embarrass you, gossip about you, keep you from getting work done, or verbally abuse you.

This is incredibly disappointing, given that as you climb the ladder of success, you are more likely to be a threat to insecure people who are desperate to hold onto their fragile psyches and maintain control.

Thus, the more you shine, the more you will attract bullies, like moths to a flame. Prepare for battle scars likely to ensue from this encounter.

Lunch Notes

Describe a time when you were seen as a threat. What happened? #LunchNotes

(23) #Strength

Taking jujitsu was an incredibly powerful experience. Although it was mixed with many highs and lows, overall it was a great experience because I found a strength, I never knew I had.

Jujitsu put me in an incredibly uncomfortable situation. It was the most uncomfortable that I have ever been. Basically, sweaty, strange men would be on top of me, trying to choke me or break my arm off. It is a competitive sport filled with large egos. And you must engage to win—or else your opponent will basically try to murder you.

I also learned that although I was placed in incredibly difficult and uncomfortable situations—and left sometimes with bruises and a black eye—I, incredibly, never died.

I learned that I not only survived in those harsh conditions, but I also came away learning something new—win or lose. I always left the mat with new knowledge that I could apply to my next role. Thus, through adversity came tremendous growth.

The physical strength that came from participating in a physical activity and competitive sport translated into internal strength. The physical ability to defend myself translated into the mental ability to defend myself. The confidence that I gained from training in a physical sport translated into confidence in my professional life, empowering me to stand up for myself. Self-defense on the mat translated to self-defense for my career and my core values.

When has physical strength translated to emotional and mental strength? #LunchNotes

(24) #FlowerDress

I've always worn dresses, the more flowery the better. I'm sure I own one pair of pants, which I wear only when the temperature drops below freezing. Any one of my friends, my family members, my colleagues, or the random people I meet will vouch that I am beyond a girl's girl. There is not one sparkle gel pen that I do not own.

Enter the flower dress, a.k.a. my "battle dress." I don't believe in changing who you are to lean in or lean out. Wearing a pantsuit was never in my DNA, although I do admit to cutting my hair short and wearing it differently in hopes that people would take me more seriously. I'm convinced I lost a terrible amount of hair, and nothing changed.

Embracing myself was critical to ensuring my ability to prepare for battle with the acrylic-glass ceiling. My flower dress represented my femininity, and my femininity was not a negative but a positive.

I learned through my time training in jujitsu that I could not go head to head with a male opponent using the exact same tactics that he used. There was no denying that my opponent was usually bigger than me and could outmuscle me. However, as a woman, I was more flexible and had more cardio longevity. Thus, as we would go head to head during a roll, I knew all I had to do was conserve my energy, not panic when I was in a disadvantage, squirm out of close calls with my flexibility, and take an advantageous inch when I sensed exhaustion from my opponent. Once I had that inch, I would try everything to not let that inch go until I was able to take another inch. Until, inch by inch, I had placed my opponent in a rear naked choke, and I could then submit him.

Femininity does not have to be classified as a weakness, and it does not have to define you as a fragile flower. My battle dress is my flower dress, and it represents my strength, my femininity. I have found it to be advantageous to learn about my strengths as a woman and lean into them, instead of changing who I am.

Describe a time when your femininity was used as a strength. #LunchNotes

PHOTOGRAPH COURTESY OF PEXELS

(25) #KnightInShiningArmor

Why is it, as women, we are taught to wait for our knight in shining armor to save us? That we are too fragile and incapable to advocate for ourselves and fight for what we believe in?

It is possible that sometimes even our chivalrous knight in shining armor shows up wrapped in the shiny garb of benevolent sexism.

Chivalrous behavior can sometimes mask benevolent sexism. For example, your boss doesn't give you a promotion, because he thinks that a woman needs to be with her family and be available to make dinner, thus he is doing you a favor. Although this type of sexism is not hostile, it makes women feel that they are weaker and not capable of handling certain responsibilities.[14]

Taking benevolent sexism to the side for a moment. Historically speaking, if we imagine a man (who is not your father) in full-on battle gear with his weapon raised, the probability that this battle-armored man is riding toward you at lightning pace to save you is very low. He is more likely riding toward you with his blade raised to pillage your village, steal your cattle, and slaughter your pigs. I recommend if you even see a man in full-on battle gear riding towards you, you pick up your children and run the other way.

---

14 Joy D'Souza. "Chivalry Is Sexist, Says New Study." HuffPost Canada. March 11, 2015. https://www.huffingtonpost.ca/2015/03/11/chivalry-sexist_n_6847264.html.

When did you decide to stop waiting for your knight in shining armor and decided instead to save yourself? #LunchNotes

(26) #ContinuousLearning

One of the greatest gifts that my parents gave me was the ability and desire to continuously learn. They instilled such support and excitement for learning that I never wanted to stop learning after I left school.

My dad often pointed out: Don't make the deliberate decision to stop reading after you leave school. If you keep reading and you keep learning, you will never stop growing.

In fact, my most enjoyable parts of my life have been when I have sought to understand things about my life by seeking authors and thought leaders in the field of interest and by immersing myself to understand the truth.

Studying areas that I am truly interested in, whether it is social inequalities, finances, or women's issues, has filled my life with meaning and enjoyment. I can't stop reading and seeking the truth of each topic, delving deep and filling my head with wondrous information and thoughts.

Now what could be better and more enjoyable than learning without exams?

What is a topic that you find fascinating and that has filled your life with fulfillment and meaning? #LunchNotes

PHOTOGRAPH COURTESY OF UNSPLASH

(27) #FinanacialFreedom

One of the greatest lessons I learned was that independence and financial freedom were intertwined. As a modern woman, I have always identified myself as an independent woman and have put great emphasis on maintaining my independence.

This means always having the option to eject myself from a situation, whether it is a bad relationship or a bad working environment, when I want to, since my finances are stable and secure enough to support my decisions.

Taking time to empower myself by understanding my finances, including investing for my financial future, has been one of the best investments in myself.

Financial health and well-being have been the cornerstone to my ability to function as a modern, independent woman.

Taking a hard look at my money attitude and what money means to me, then taking time to read a few financial books, has been critical to my independence.

One of the first money books I read made me question why as women we tend to think that money knowledge is too hard for us and why we then blindly hand over our paychecks to our husbands. Women perform well academically, so then why do we think money knowledge is harder than calculus? The book then made me ask: Why do we think that men make better family financial decisions even though traditional gender roles suggest that women tend to think of the family instead of only themselves when making decisions? This line of questioning also made me wonder what my husband would do if we were both magically given access to $10,000. In the name of science, I asked him this hypothetical scenario. I told him that I would pay off the debt we owed. He told me that he would buy a boat, but obviously the boat would be shared between the two of us. The line of questioning only reinforced the need to increase my knowledge of money and my confidence when it came to money matters.

Some first steps included learning about individual retirement accounts (IRAs), thrift savings plans (TSPs), and stocks and readjusting my money attitude so that I paid myself first (automatically depositing into my TSP with each paycheck). Empowering myself with money knowledge provided me the support I needed to make sure that I was never trapped in a situation that I couldn't leave. I have seen single mothers suffer abusive behaviors at work because they lived paycheck to paycheck, I have seen women stay in abusive marriages because they depended on their spouse for financial support, and I myself have worked in a job where I had to keep my mouth shut since my superior held power over my paycheck. This is not a good feeling to have, this feeling of helplessness. I was determined to break free of this cycle by building up the knowledge and resources I needed.

What are steps that you have taken to empower yourself towards the goal of financial freedom? #LunchNotes

(28) #MagicalBeard

HARRISON RANDALL, PHARMD
SCIENTIST & RESEARCHER

The results from last year's workplace survey were in: 3 percent of employees in my organization were younger than thirty. At the time of my writing, I am nearing my late twenties, but my beard makes me look older.

My past life as a clean-shaven individual was rough. As a member of the 3 percent, I stuck out like a sore thumb in office meetings. I was often the youngest person in the room by at least a decade, and as such, I was often assumed to be an intern rather than a full-time employee. Outside of the office, it was often assumed that I was a college student rather than a licensed professional with a doctoral degree. (In all fairness to the world, my clean-shaven self does look like a teenager.) I have, of course, mitigated this problem by embracing facial hair. In addition to being taken more seriously in the workplace, I am no longer asked to show identification to receive alcoholic beverages. It's magical.

The evolutionary reason for facial hair has been speculated since the days of Darwin.[15] Is it to protect one's face from the elements? Is it to attract mates? Is it to intimidate competitors? Maybe all of the above and then some. Regardless of the primal reasons for its existence, the beard has psychological implications in today's world. A 2012 study involved showing pictures of bearded and clean-shaven male faces to a diverse group of men and women and asking participants to guess the age and social "importance" of each photographed face. The bearded faces were rated as having higher social status and being of older age than the clean-shaven faces.[16]

15 Charles Darwin. "The Descent of Man, and Selection in Relation to Sex." 1871. https://doi:10.5962/bhl.title.121292.

16 Barnaby J. Dixson and Paul L. Vasey. "Beards Augment Perceptions of Men's Age, Social Status, and Aggressiveness, but Not Attractiveness." Behavioral Ecology 23, no. 3 (January 13, 2012): 481-90. doi:10.1093/beheco/arr214.

And there was my scientific evidence that a beard could make me appear older and more distinguished.

Age discrimination in employment is legally prohibited, so long as one is at least forty years of age.[17] Such laws are sensible, given that employers may otherwise see older adults as a disadvantage to productivity. However, the aging workforce of today leaves insufficient evidence to support such beliefs.[18] Nearly 70 percent of the more than seventeen thousand employees in my organization are forty or older; this percentage is not far removed from nationwide estimates of older employees in the US workforce.[19] Let me rephrase these facts: more than one third of US workers are younger than forty years of age, yet it is not against federal law for employers to discriminate against these individuals based on age.

A youthful workforce has its benefits. A 2017 study of nearly nineteen thousand physicians in the United States found that patients treated by older physicians had higher mortality rates than those treated by younger physicians.[20] As a healthcare professional working in an environment saturated with other healthcare professionals, I was not surprised by the results of this study. It is rare to find someone who, after decades of working in a given field, still cares about professional excellence, still cares about serving others, and isn't afraid to unlearn outdated information. (As I will explain later, those rare individuals who *do* still care are people who deserve your utmost respect and whom you should adopt as mentors). Improving oneself every day takes a lot of effort and is therefore not a goal that most people pursue,

---

17 U.S. Equal Employment Opportunity Commission. The Age Discrimination in Employment Act of 1967. 1967. https://www.eeoc.gov/laws/statutes/adea.cfm

18 Burtless, Gary. "The Impact of Population Aging and Delayed Retirement on Workforce Productivity." 2013. Center for Retirement Research at Boston College. http://crr.bc.edu/wp-content/uploads/2013/05/wp_2013-111.pdf

19 Richard Fry. "Millennials are the Largest Generation in the U.S. Labor Force." Pew Research Center. April 11, 2018. http://www.pewresearch.org/fact-tank/2018/04/11/millennials-largest-generation-us-labor-force/

20 Yusuke Tsugawa, Joseph P. Newhouse, Alan M. Zaslavsky, Daniel M. Blumenthal, and Anupam B. Jena. "Physician Age and Outcomes in Elderly Patients in Hospital in the US: Observational Study." BMJ, May 16, 2017. Accessed March 11, 2019. doi:10.1136/bmj.j1797.

let alone achieve, for years on end. It is much easier to *appear* mature than to *be* mature. It is much easier to grow a beard.

A common stereotype is that younger age means less experience. This is true in the strictest sense—that age correlates with a greater *quantity* of experiences—but it is frustrating when it is used to assume anything about the *quality* or relevance of those experiences. Technology moves faster now, and so too does the world around it. We millennials have been raised using technologies that did not exist or were in a primitive state not long before we were born. As such technologies—social media, mobile apps, and so on—continue to be adopted into the mainstream, every organization tries to capitalize on them or risk becoming obsolete. Who is best suited to integrate these technologies into a corporate structure that has stood for decades or longer? Assigning that responsibility to the key stakeholders within the organization—the young people—is a risk. It hands the reins to employees who can best understand the problem and envision possible solutions but who have the least seniority in the workplace. It disrupts the hierarchy. Young people might have the *quality* of experience, but not necessarily the *quantity* of experience necessary to be trusted by the true decision-makers. Age carries the benefit of understanding the problem, and it bears the curse of not being positioned to have creative control over the solution.

I recognize that growing a magical beard is not a plausible solution for everyone. Thankfully, there are other stylistic choices that have their own fantastical powers. Eyeglasses are a more gender-neutral example that come with their own stereotype of making the wearer appear more intelligent. If you are a fellow glasses-wearer, then you will be pleased to know that this stereotype is supported by evidence.[21] In the healthcare field, many young practitioners swear that long white coats magically confer an air of authority, or at least make it more difficult for those around the practitioners to ignore the credentials that are visibly embroidered across the chest. Additionally, I would be remiss to not mention the effects of cosmetics, which has been shown to effectively

---

21 Forster Leder and Gerger. "The Glasses Stereotype Revisited." Swiss Journal of Psychology, 2011. https://doi.org/10.1024/1421-0185/a000059

make younger women appear older and older women appear younger.[22] These examples are symbolic of the superficial changes that every young professional can make to appear more deserving of respect.

At some point in your life, maybe after a breakup with a significant other, you were probably told, "Don't change yourself for other people." Is this advice still true?

If someone really does have something against you for reasons you cannot change—age, race, gender, and so on—they will not change their opinions because you grew a beard. They will always find something wrong with you. They will never be pleased. We all make superficial changes, sometimes at great expense, to affect how the people around us perceive us, but we have to be mindful that we are changing ourselves for the right reasons. Change yourself to improve your own confidence. Wear glasses if they make you feel intelligent. Wear clothes that make you feel impressive. Do these things because they please *you*. If you maximize your own self-confidence, you will be more likely to act with ambition. You will be more likely to advocate for yourself and stand up for what you know to be true. You will be more likely to make decisions that befit such a smart, stylish person who will run the world one day, and you will be more likely to surround yourself with people who are equally motivated to achieve success. If you behave this way every day, you will develop a reputation. You will become known for the traits you personify. You will start to be taken seriously by people who can help you achieve your goals. *That* is magical.

You have undoubtedly encountered problems in your workplace that have led you to say, "Things would be so much better if I were in charge." Maybe that is true—maybe you could run the show better than anyone else, or perhaps you just have good ideas that current leadership should implement for the benefit of all. Regardless, it is difficult to accomplish such aims without assistance from other like-minded individuals. If you are serious about reaching your goals, you must seek mentorship from people who have already achieved success and ally yourself with those who epitomize the personal and professional traits

---

22 Russell et al. "Differential Effects of Makeup on Perceived Age." British Journal of Psychology, 2018. https://doi.org/10.1111/bjop.12337

that you seek. When you improve yourself and develop a positive reputation, you will magically begin to meet equally hard-working people.

Young professionals do not benefit from being surrounded solely by other young professionals. Swinging the pendulum too far in favor of young employees is problematic, as recognized by the current state of the tech industry, in which older employees fear losing their jobs due to age and will take drastic steps to appear younger. Yet in that same field, younger employees realize how beneficial it is to have more senior employees in the workplace.[23] We benefit from mentorship by older professionals who have already achieved success but continue to push their boundaries and reach greater heights. A good mentor is the key to both personal and professional growth, so long as they can speak from experience. They must have experienced ups and downs and successes and failures, and they must be honest enough to acknowledge their good and bad decisions. Only then will they be able to call you out when *you* make bad decisions and provide you with tough love when you need it. A good mentor within your organization will help to make up for certain disadvantages you may face as a young professional. They will stake their reputation to vouch for you, which will magically reveal career opportunities that were otherwise invisible.

I still like my magical beard. However, I realize that, like all good magic, there is a hidden reason why the illusion works. It has very little to do with the beard—though the scientifically demonstrated benefits are a nice bonus—and very much to do with how I changed as a person and a professional. I improved myself, which improved my quality of work, which led to professional relationships with other ambitious and hard-working people, which opened new opportunities for career advancement. I am still at the beginning of my career, but thanks to the advice of people much smarter, savvier, and more successful than me, the path ahead is clearer. And as of now, those people advise me to keep the beard.

23 Raj Mukherjee. 2017. "Report: Ageism in the Tech Industry." Indeed Blog. December 27, 2018. http://blog.indeed.com/2017/10/19/tech-ageism-report/.

Does your age define how people treat you?
Describe your experiences. #LunchNotes

PHOTOGRAPH COURTESY OF RAW PIXEL

(29) #SaleOfYourSoul

I am often amazed how quickly and cheaply people sell their souls. Transactions are often made at a highly discounted, and sometimes even negative, rate.

We see this at times when a promotion is at stake and people may steal, lie, threat, harass, or throw others under the bus. Additionally, when people see others getting ahead by using these cheap tricks, some start to follow. This pattern is similar to when a husband abuses his wife, and the children eventually join in on the abuse of their mother. Research shows that children who see fathers abuse their mothers absorb the abuser's messages that their mother has traits deserving of the abuse, and they may gradually come to look down on their mother as a parent and participate in the abusive behavior.[24]

Be aware, this is a greased slope. According to Albert Bandura's social-cognitive theory and moral disengagement theory, deceitful conduct usually starts with repeated, small indiscretions that eventually escalate to more severe incidents.[25] For example, someone who steals a car typically does not start with stealing cars. The indiscretions typically start small, such as stealing small items like cosmetics, moving up to possibly an iPhone, then to stealing laptops, and then to car theft.

As such, once you start on the sale of your soul, the more greased and inclined the slope gets. Folklore dictates that once your soul is sold, there is very little chance of it coming back.

---

24 Eileen Fletcher. "So Where Does It Begin?" Unhealthy Relationships. March 01, 2017. Accessed March 15, 2019. https://unhealthyrelationships.wordpress.com/verbal-abuse/begin/.

25 Albert Bandura. Selective moral disengagement in the exercise of moral agency. Journal of moral education. Vol 31 (2), 2002. https://web.stanford.edu/~kcarmel/CC_BehavChange_Course/readings/Additional%20Resources/Bandura/bandura_moraldisengagement.pdf

Have you witnessed others selling their soul at a discounted or even negative rate? #LunchNotes

PHOTOGRAPH COURTESY OF RAW PIXEL

(30) #BabyAlphas

AURORA SKYY, PHD
SCIENTIST & RESEARCHER

The blowup T. rex costume is incredibly entertaining. With the floppy body and little T. rex arms, it makes everything comedic. We have seen YouTube videos of parents embarrassing their kids at the school bus stop, parents chasing their embarrassed offspring in their clumsy T. rex bodies, and others skateboarding with the T. rex arms flailing around. (For the readers who may have been too young to remember this phase in our generation's life, I highly recommend seeking out a "vintage" video.) Unfortunately, the baby alphas in the workplace are not as comedic or entertaining.

Baby alphas are typically newly minted young women in managing positions who hyper exert their authority. They are extremely territorial and find the need to intimidate all other women into submission. They usually find immense satisfaction in pointing out every little error, putting made-up barriers in your way, and using aggressive stances in their body language. Yes, you are now all thinking about that one person. I will pause here to give you time to imagine them in the blowup T. rex costume.

Next time this baby alpha exaggerates her status to increase her superiority complex over you, I can guarantee that she will hold little, if any, power over you once you picture her in her T. rex blowup costume. It's my gift to you.

Describe the baby alpha at your workplace. How does she overexert her power? #LunchNotes

(31) #BoundFeet

YIZHOUS "JAMES" YE, PHD
SCIENTIST & RESEARCHER

Are you familiar with the history of little Chinese girls getting their feet bound? This practice was extremely brutal. But even more heartbreaking was that women who had their own feet bound would be the ones binding the feet of little girls.

Instead of denying this torturous and barbaric act that was inflicted on them and preventing the same trauma from being done to others, these women would hold down the little girls and make them suffer through what they had suffered.

We see this in modern-day society when women who have gotten to the top with many battle scars become bullies to other women because they feel the need to have other women suffer what they have suffered.

When women bully other women, this makes me incredibly sad because this typically comes from a place of insecurity and jealousy. They not only see you as a threat to their baby-alpha territory but feel that since they were bullied to get to where they are at, they need to make you feel their pain and suffering also. They will typically revert to traditional bully behavior to ensure maximum suffering,

Instead of using their experience to reach back and pull you up and help you avoid land mines, they drop land mines behind them to make sure that you too will feel the pain of walking in the glass slipper.

Instead of forming an old boys' club, like men tend to do, bully women tend not to see power in numbers, and instead they turn into baby alphas, fighting other woman off their turf.

I disagree with this mentality of having younger women suffer the same pains as the women before them. If the women before me (grandmothers, aunts, mothers, and so on) had not fought for the current generation of women, they would probably would still be pouring coffee for the men in their office. However, just because the women of today, no longer must pour coffee for the men in their office, does not mean that they have a challenge-free workplace. This means that the modern-day woman can focus on other challenges that arise (#AcrylicGlassCeiling, etc.), so that the generation behind them can take another step up.

Share a story about a time when you were made to feel the pain that others experienced before you. #LunchNotes

PHOTOGRAPH COURTESY OF RAW PIXEL

(32) #Haters

Some people (small-minded people) will root for you to fail. It is inevitable. Haters will intensify their tricks against you the more successful you get.

Interestingly enough and be aware, the haters typically become to act like your new best buddies and your number-one fans and supporters once you show a certain level of success. Then your success becomes their success, as they will very likely try to claim credit or take advantage of your newly elevated status.

Can you convince haters to stop hating you? Unfortunately, haters are usually determined to stay unhappy with others' success. It is impossible to stop haters being haters.

But it helps to think of the haters as just noise. They will continue making noise in order to distract you from success. Isolating out the noise and focusing only on your step-by-step progression is crucial. Energy spent on the haters is energy taken away from your ability to move forward.

Lunch Notes

When have you experienced haters? What was the reason? #LunchNotes

(33) #MiddleSchoolMeanies

According to psychologist Jennifer Newman and supported by literature, high-performing employees are more likely to get bullied at work. Employees with high cognitive ability and those who work exceptionally hard can experience more victimization.[26] Newman suggests that the risk of workplace bullying is greater for highly competent employees who reliably produce good work.

Bullies typically have two traits that lead them into engaging in their bully behavior: 1) awareness of high performers' traits and 2) an inflated opinion of their own contributions.[27]

Jennifer Newman notes that when a bully's insecurities are threatened and feelings of inferiorities surface, these lead to feelings of shame, humiliation, envy, and jealousy and an increase in resentment and hostility towards the high performer. Hostility and resentment can take place as the following:

1. **Undermining** (e.g., everyone hates your work)
2. **Domination** (e.g., I've been here for longer, so I deserve X and you don't, so you stay in your swim lane)
3. **Sabotage** (spreading malicious lies)
4. **Workplace mobbing** (group bullying, repeated and focused efforts to negatively target a top performer to get them to leave the organization—a.k.a. bullying on steroids)

Jennifer Newman states in her work that bullies engage in these behaviors as an effort to restore their damaged self-image. By harming the high-performing colleague, they attempt to restore and maintain their good opinion of themselves. Bullying typically persists and increases

26 About. Dr. Jennifer Newman, R.Psych. http://drjennifernewman.com/about-vancouver-psychologist/

27 Newman, Jennifer. "High Performers Victimized at Work." April 6 2017. http://drjennifernewman.com/2017/04/high-performers-victimized-at-work/

in aggression, as the restoration of the bully's self-image by harming another is only a temporary fix.

Workplace mobbing is a particularly effective and increasingly common bullying tactic. This can be considered an extreme form of workplace competition, where employees join forces to ostracize, marginalize, and ultimately eliminate their perceived competition. This type of behavior has been documented in research for decades.[28] In a classic study by Melville Dalton,[29] the researcher noted that this practice of workplace mobbing occurs when the group views the top performers as "rate busters." Many times, in a workplace, there is an unspoken and informal consensus that only *X* amount of productivity will be accepted. But top performers refuse to be held back by this group norm. Typically, these "rate busters" were just responding to incentives placed by leaders to perform highly, and as a result they are harassed, threatened, and sometimes physically harmed by their coworkers, all because they refused to conform to peer pressure to underperform.

Besides being rate busters, anyone who is different from the organizational norm can be a target, according to psychologist Sophie Henshaw.[30] Usually victims are competent, educated, resilient, outspoken, challenging of the status quo, and more empathic or attractive, and they tend to be women aged thirty-two to fifty-five. Targets also can be racially different or part of a minority group.[31] Regardless of the reason for being a rate buster or just being different, the process begins when a group of instigators decides to case someone, under the pretext that the victim is threatening their interest (whatever it may be). Mobsters' weapon of choice for elimination is negative communication, including

---

28 Pamela Lutgen-Sandvik, Sarah J. Tracy, and Jess K. Alberts. "Burned by Bullying in the American Workplace: Prevalence, Perception, Degree and Impact." Journal of Management Studies 44 (6): 837–62. https://doi.org/10.1111/j.1467-6486.2007.00715.x.

29 Dalton, Melville. "'The Industrial 'Rate Buster': A Characterization." Human Organization 7 (1): 5–18. https://doi.org/10.17730/humo.7.1.f461ht3145154752.

30 Henshaw, Sophie. "Bullying at Work: Workplace Mobbing Is on the Rise." PsychCentral. July 8, 2018. https://psychcentral.com/blog/bullying-at-work-workplace-mobbing-is-on-the-rise/.

31 Henshaw, Sophie. "Bullying at Work: Workplace Mobbing Is on the Rise." PsychCentral. July 8, 2018. https://psychcentral.com/blog/bullying-at-work-workplace-mobbing-is-on-the-rise/.

anonymous complaints, gossip, hearsay, defamation, and twisting the story to frame the target as a troublemaker or a bully.

The results are devastating: the victim is left reeling from confusion and may experience severe anxiety, PTSD, and even suicide.[32]

These statistics about what increases the risk of being targeted at work make me incredibly sad. As parents or future parents, we all hope that our children will grow up to be bright, healthy, empathetic souls. Yet decades of shaping our children and guiding them with values of hard work, helping them strive to be the best and contribute meaningfully to society, places them at increased risk of harm; in order to survive the workplace jungle, they need to reduce productivity, decrease their light, decrease empathy, and preferably not be attractive.

Most of us have experienced middle-school meanie behavior. Unfortunately, this behavior can be exacerbated in the workplace, given that we never have the escape of "graduating" middle school in the workplace.

---

32 Eve Seguin. "Academic Mobbing, or How to Become Campus Tormentors." University Affairs. September 19, 2016. https://www.universityaffairs.ca/opinion/in-my-opinion/academic-mobbing-become-campus-tormentors/.

Have you experienced middle school meanies? #LunchNotes

(34) #ZeroSumGame

JOHN HARIADI, MD
PHYSICIAN

In a zero-sum game, there is only one winner. Thus, the other person must lose, as the world total can only equal zero. Winner (+ 1), loser (-1) = zero.

This is unfortunately sometimes incorrectly translated into life, in which people believe that if you win, it means they will have to lose. In reality, there is no magical fixed number of winners in life. Yes, everyone can win!

What typically happens instead is that if your coworker or friend wins, then your network gets stronger. If your relationships are genuine and strong, then when your network grows stronger, typically you will also get stronger. This is the idea of synergy: the interaction or cooperation of two or more entities to produce a combined effect greater than the sum of their separate effects. Synergy is a real phenomenon. We see it in everyday life, from business (complementary firms teaming up to grow faster) to nature (like how bees feed from the flowers they in turn pollinate).

Life is rarely a binary choice, a simple yes-or-no decision. Finding that win-win may take a bit more effort, but invariably it is there if you look for it.

If you do not believe in the zero-sum game, you will see your allies winning and your network growing stronger. This in turn will open doors to opportunities for all of you. And you can all be winners.

Describe a win-win situation. #LunchNotes

PHOTOGRAPH COURTESY OF RAW PIXEL

(35) #OldBoysClub

I'm going to share with you my crib notes about the old boys' club battle strategies on silencing and suppressing a noncompliant woman.

I hope that sharing these strategies with you takes away the power of their manipulation and bully techniques. Like a cheap magic trick, once you know what is behind the curtain, it loses all its powers.

Thankfully the battle strategies to force a woman into submission are limited. Unfortunately, these battle strategies are extremely effective, and typically not all techniques need to be used before a woman gives up.

It helps to visualize these old boys' club battle techniques written on a tattered, grease-stained dinner napkin sitting pathetically on your bedside table.

I present below my notes on the old boys' club submission techniques and some suggestions on how to defeat them.

Technique 1: Dismiss a woman's claims. Say she is too sensitive or emotional. This is the most commonly used technique to silence a woman from trying to assert herself and stand up for herself. It is typically what I like to call an "undertone technique," in that it is not apparent, but it is effective. Think of the air being removed from the room. You know something is amiss, but you can't really put your finger on it, so you shut down.

Additionally, this technique reinforces the stereotypes that women are emotionally unstable, dramatic, and overly sensitive. We accept these stereotypes; thus, when a bully points out these characteristics, we tend to believe them. We shut down our internal voice to stand up for ourselves and question whether our stance was important. We give power over to the bully and question our claim. Typically, at this point we can choose to maintain power and assert our claim. If you are dealing with an emotionally stable person, this is all that is needed. However, if your bully is one who is highly insecure or has learned that they have been successful in suppressing a noncompliant woman using additional techniques, then be prepared for the bully to move to the second battle technique.

Technique 2: Use aggression and humiliation techniques. These forms of submission techniques include speaking over you, using loud voices, swearing at you, eye-rolling, aggressive posturing and publicly humiliating you. All these techniques are meant to intimidate you into submission in your gender role.

Or they can be of the microaggression type. Microaggressions are common in the workplace because they are hard to point out and because typically only the victim is aware of such behaviors. These microaggressions can include not making eye contact with you in meetings, turning their body away from you, and being extremely critical of your work. Hypercritical behavior is a very effective manipulation and control technique because it can be passed off as the bully trying to help you. However, pointing out that you have an extra space or a random typo in your writing is a method to show that the bully is superior, and you are inferior. This inferiority complex that the bully is developing in you is typically enough to destroy your confidence and ability to stand up for yourself.

Technique 3: Say the woman lied or falsely accuse her. This technique will typically scare the woman away because she will quickly calculate that she does not have the energy to prove her innocence, unlike typical criminal cases in which the perpetrator is innocent until proven guilty. You immediately stack the odds against this noncompliant woman by putting the onus on her and turning her into the guilty party. Having this onus put on the noncompliant woman will usually push her back into her socially acceptable role and teach her to not disturb you again by standing up for herself. The thought that she is the guilty party for daring to speak up for herself will typically send her to tears and return the power back to the bully immediately because often the woman has already used the last of her inner strength to come forward to fight for her rights. Accusing her of lying will typically send her into a chasm and punish her for standing up for herself. This technique is usually all that is needed for the bully to win, and most victims give up once someone uses this technique.

This is a type of psychological manipulation called *gaslighting*. The term *gaslighting* came from the 1940s movie *Gaslight*. In the movie, the husband, wanting to inherit his wife's money, starts manipulating small things around her. When the wife starts questioning these small changes, the husband continually denies it and insists that she is delusional, and the wife starts questioning her sanity. Gaslighting is a very effective way to manipulate someone's perception of reality and disorient the victim.[33]

My personal experience is that if you are accused of lying, remember that the truth always surfaces. You must just hang on, as the truth when it is surfacing will be bumpy. This is when the bully will typically engage and double down on technique number 4.

Technique 4: Form an old boys' club gang. Bullies will typically support other bullies and call upon their quid pro quo in times of need. We can learn from this behavior ourselves and form a protective group-support shield against the bully behavior. Additionally, there is strength in numbers, as a single woman standing up for herself unfortunately can be martyred. If possible, I recommend creating a workgroup to systematically address the issue and recommend policy change.

Technique 5: Isolate the victim. This technique is one of the most heartbreaking and most effective techniques to force a noncompliant woman into submission. This is because women are typically social beings and support is immensely important to their daily functioning. Removing a woman's support, socially alienating her as the black sheep, and turning everyone against her is extremely effective. This is typically done through gossip, character assassination, and putting fear into those who choose to align with the targeted woman. This is typically when the following terms may surface to label the noncompliant woman: *crazy*, *active imagination*, or *delusional*.

---

33 George Simon. Manipulation and the Gaslighting Effect. August 18, 2017. https://www.drgeorgesimon.com/manipulation-and-the-gaslighting-effect/

If the bully is well versed in this isolation technique, then they can turn those closest to the woman against her through gaslighting techniques. Using this psychological manipulation, the bully will sow seeds of doubt into the woman's closest friends, making them question their own memory, perception, and sanity so that those who know her will start to see her as the evil character the bully wants her to be.

Removing all support and turning her closest allies against her will typically not only force a woman back into her socially acceptable role but punish her enough to leave lasting scars so that she will remember her punishment enough to not stand up for herself again.

To survive this technique, you need several countermoves. Some may be in your control, and others may not. Your relationships and networks need to be strong enough to withstand this onslaught. Your coworkers, friends, and others who stand by you must be of high character integrity and have strong judgment. This is incredibly rare, and if you have the fortune of knowing these people of high moral and character integrity, then keep them close to you, and protect them because life can be unkind.

Additionally, you must maintain high levels of morale and character integrity through the onslaught. The bully will throw lie after lie at you to destroy your character and turn your closest friends against you. You must not lie or sink to their level of bad behavior. Maintain your integrity and character because they become your Teflon coating. The lies that are thrown at you will then merely slide off you because it is hard for lies to stick without evidence. Hunker down with your Teflon coating, and watch the lies slide off your protective shield. Eventually, the bully will get frustrated that their defamatory lies are not sticking, and they will move to another technique.

However, at this time, damage will be done, and you will exit this stage with battle wounds. Your professional reputation will most likely have changed. You will have those who will believe the bully's lies, and you can do nothing but maintain course. Additionally, some of your personal relationships will be damaged, and some closest to you will have turned against you. However, at the same time, your relationships with those who stood by you will have been transformed into a level of trust, respect, and strength that is rarely seen. Hopefully your faith in humanity and in truth triumphing over evil will be reconfirmed. Remember, your battle gear is not just a flower dress but an impenetrable, invisible shield of integrity and support.

Technique 6: Turning into the victim. This technique is used typically as a last resort by the bully. I find it immensely entertaining when this technique is used because this means that you have survived all other bully techniques and you just need to have this one play out. I find that once the victim card is played, the bully will typically quit, as he has run out of manipulation tools.

My recommendation is to sit back and enjoy watching this technique unfold while the bully starts accusing you of all the behaviors that they have inflicted on you, saying that you are the aggressor. The bully will typically play the pitiful victim and try to sway others to side with them as a victim.

However, since you have your Teflon coating of integrity, the bully will have no evidence that you have done anything. Accusing you of things you have not done and turning themselves into the victim is ridiculous, and you must resist giving any of these behaviors or words any weight. They are lifeless without any backing or evidence.

Sit back and enjoy the show, as it may include sniffling, tears, wailing, name-calling, and finger-pointing—anything to distract from the bully's own behaviors and force the attention onto you. Eventually, if no weight is given to the bully's accusation and victim role playing, and no evidence is presented, the bully will look like the fool for making up lies, and their own reputation will be affected, as now they will be seen as a dramatic, belligerent person and a liar. Popcorn, anyone?

I provide my notes on the battle techniques to arm you with knowledge.

Once these techniques are exposed, like a cheap magic trick, they lose their power over you.

What other old boys' club techniques have you experienced? Share them. #LunchNotes

(36) #PigtailPulling

I had originally naively thought that sexual harassment was just awkward flirting and weird foreplay from an awkward man. But I was wrong. This was not awkward flirting by an awkward man. It was about power.

Catharine MacKinnon, a prominent legal theorist, points out that sexual harassment is really an abuse of power, with or without explicit sexual behavior.[34]

Take, for example, a man catcalling a woman in the streets. How often does catcalling bring a woman towards the man? I will say it is not often that a woman will approach the man whistling at her and making jeering remarks like "Hey, baby. Nice ass."

Instead, very likely it forces the woman to increase her pace and walk to the other side of the street. That was power the man had, to remove the woman from her space and force her to cross the street. He had control over where she walked and allowed to physically exist. That is power.

In the workplace when a harasser sabotages a woman's work (I also like to call this behavior *pigtail pulling*), he is not engaging in any type of romantic sexual action. This is not an engagement of affection, not unlike the street harasser who comments on a woman's body as she walks by. When a harasser sabotages a woman's work, he is controlling where she can function and exist in the workplace.

Confusion about the difference between sexual invitation and sexual harassment is common. For example: Is he pulling my pigtail because he has a crush on me, or is it something else? The difference between invitation and harassment is the use of power. Harassment is not a form of courtship, and it is not meant to appeal to women. It is designed to coerce women, not to attract them. Affection becomes

34 Catherine A. MacKinnon. Sexual Harassment of Working Women. New Haven and London, Yale University Press, 1976.

aggression when the recipient loses her ability to consent without fear of the consequences.[35]

"Women tend to be economically valued according to men's perceptions of their potential to be sexually harassed," MacKinnon argues. "They are, in effect, required to 'ask for it.'" The concept of the "wife mother" was brought up by sociologist Talcott Parsons, in which a woman's role was divided into three main tasks: (1) ego-stroking, (2) housekeeping (e.g., administrative tasks), and (3) role of a "sex object."[36]

When I was younger, whenever a man gave me the once-over (aka elevator eyes), I would feel icky inside. But I did not understand why, as I was confused. Was this a form of flattery? If so, why the uncomfortable feeling? However, I learned later that it was a method for harassers to disarm me and remind me of my sex.[37] "Sexual harassment is a subtle rape, and rape is more about fear than sex," said Dr. John Gottman, a psychologist at the University of Washington. "Harassment is a way for a man to make a woman vulnerable."[38]

Psychologist Jennifer Newman has written in her work how independent, assertive women with leadership qualities are more likely to be sexually harassed.[39] As noted by Catherine MacKinnon, sexual harassment is motivated to punish women who blur the gender lines, rather than being motivated by sexual desire.[40] Additionally, moral philosopher Kate Manne, argues that "misogyny should not be understood primarily in terms of the hatred or hostility some men feel toward all or

---

35 Martha J. Langelan. Back off!: How to Confront and Stop Sexual Harassment and Harassers. New York: Simon & Schuster, 1993.

36 "Talcott Parsons." Sociologyguide.com. Accessed March 15, 2019. http://www.sociologyguide.com/thinkers/Talcott-Parsons.php.

37 Ginia Bellafante. 2018. "Before #MeToo, There Was Catharine A. MacKinnon and Her Book 'Sexual Harassment of Working Women.'" The New York Times. The New York Times. March 19, 2018. https://www.nytimes.com/2018/03/19/books/review/metoo-workplace-sexual-harassment-catharine-mackinnon.html.

38 Daniel Goleman. "Sexual Harassment: It's About Power, Not Lust." The New York Times. The New York Times. October 22, 1991. https://www.nytimes.com/1991/10/22/science/sexual-harassment-it-s-about-power-not-lust.html.

39 Jennifer Newman. "Assertive Women are More Likely to be Sexually Harassed at Work." March 3, 2018. http://drjennifernewman.com/2018/03/assertive-women-are-more-likely-to-be-sexually-harassed-at-work/.

40 Catherine A. MacKinnon. Sexual Harassment of Working Women. New Haven and London, Yale University Press. 1976.

most women. Rather, it's primarily about controlling, policing, punishing, and exiling the "bad" women who challenge male dominance. And it's compatible with rewarding "the good ones," and singling out other women to serve as warnings to those who are out of order."[41]

In many sexual harassment cases, following the woman's refusal, the man retaliates by using his power over her job or career. Retaliation comes in many forms: losing out on a promotion, being labeled a troublemaker, getting demoted, having unfavorable materials be solicited and put in a personal file, or being placed on disciplinary layoff. Sudden allegations of job incompetence and poor attitude commonly follow rejections of sexual advances and are used to support employment consequences. Women whose work has been praised and encouraged suddenly find themselves accused of incompetence or of sabotaging their employer's projects and blamed for any downturn in business fortunes.[42]

Understanding the minutia and the psychology of sexual harassment and misogyny and its linkage to power is critical for the modern professional woman. In today's world, where the undertones are strong enough to derail a woman, she must be prepared to defend herself and arm herself with knowledge, so that she does not waste precious time in a confused state.

41 Kate Manne. Down Girl. The logic of Misogyny. Oxford University Press. 2018

42 Catherine A. MacKinnon. Sexual Harassment of Working Women. New Haven and London, Yale University Press. 1976.

Describe what the word power means to you. #LunchNotes

THE POWER OF WE

ART BY KIMBRA G. TURNER PHD

(37) #PowerOfWe

I am blessed with an amazing support group and I want you have one too. This book was created to provide a platform for you to share your story and gain emotional support from others. To give significance to your experiences, to continue conversations, bring awareness to topics, and raise these important issues to the surface. By bringing people together in shared experiences, we want to show that you are not alone, as well as collectively provide shared strategies as we grow together in this journey

The Power of We is not an us-against-them mentality, but rather a movement that includes everyone: husbands, parents, leadership, coworkers, and friends who all believe in social justice, respect, fair treatment, and smashing through all the glass analogies.

The ladder in my story, holding me up to the glass ceiling, is not made of wood or metal. It's the support of my parents, husband, son, leaders, male and female friends, and coworkers.

I would not be here today, standing as a proud woman that I have become, without the vision of the #PowerOfWe movement, which will embrace and empower all of us to create a better society.

Share a story in which the "power of we" lifted you up and helped you overcome your adversity. #LunchNotes

(38) #LetMeFixYourCrown

KATIE LEUNG
TEACHER

I have been thinking a lot about my female friendships lately. Ever since I became a teenager, it has always been difficult for me to maintain friendships with other women. I don't doubt that a lot of it has to do with how judgmental society is toward women in general, which in turn makes us judgmental of each other. And for a long time, it was easier to "play the game" than it was to be true to myself first. It only gets harder when you become a mother: every decision you make—to breast- or bottle-feed, to vaccinate or not vaccinate, to buy brand-name baby clothes or buy second-hand, to attend a Montessori school or attend public school—it is all up for scrutiny. It's a tough world out there, and while I wholeheartedly believe that "the future is female," I also know that the sort of future I'm foreseeing will not happen unless we take care of each other as women first.

I saw a meme that read: "Be the woman who fixes another woman's crown without telling the world it was crooked." I've loved it ever since because it's the truth that I want to remember for myself and for all other women in my life. "Crookedness" can be temporary if we choose to treat it that way, if we expect our friends to treat us as if we're always wearing our straightest, brightest crowns, and if we open our hearts to each other's truths while kindly setting our own limits. If we never honor each other's light—and I mean the light we have, as well as the light we cannot yet see—we are guilty of letting a sister walk this earth with a crooked crown. To take pleasure in that is to also wear our own crowns superficially, and none of that will save this world, which in itself is already crooked.

When I first read the meme, it made me think shamefully about a time when I was weak and reveled in another woman's insecurity to boost my own. My ex and I had been married five or six years, and I was just coming up for air with the kids having finished breastfeeding. I was feeling more "cow" than courageous, had body-image issues, and was lonely after a couple of years of him traveling everywhere. I'm sociable and extroverted when I want to be, and I was hungry for attention. We had made dinner plans with another friend of mine; the husband got along great with my ex, and admittedly, I had a small crush on him too, simply because he'd "made eyes" at me a couple of times, and I had felt noticed. The wife was not exactly friendly. She was shy by nature, but I branded that as her insecurity. Her crown imperfectly tipped to the side, and while I tried my best to chat with her, I knew in my heart I'd taken advantage of this "weakness."

The four of us sat at the end of a long table, and I ordered a cocktail. "Eyes-Maker" kept looking up, since he had conveniently placed himself across from me, and he let his hand linger on mine when passing the appetizer tray. I was pretty sure "Shy Friend," who sat next to him, noticed, but in that moment, I selfishly chose my need for attention over her same need for an attentive husband, so when he asked to try my drink, I willingly passed it to him, returning that slight, lingering touch. I started fantasizing about how the rest of the night would go. It was nothing scandalous, but like an idiot, I visualized more eyes-making, longer lingering grazes, and perhaps even a close goodnight hug.

I underestimated Shy Friend's meekness. She immediately pointed out that she had ordered the same cocktail, and if he wanted to try it, he could and should have tried hers instead of mine. Shy Friend suddenly became my assertive friend, and that simple statement jolted me back to reality. I realized that she needed exactly what I needed—attention, love, closeness—and that I hadn't even considered how long she had been without it, because I was thinking of my own lack of attention, tallying up years of loneliness and combining that with her shyness to somehow justify my actions. What she needed the most was what I failed to give: empathy. By taking advantage of the situation Eyes-Maker put me in, I was invalidating all of her attempts, all of her efforts she had been giving to her own marriage, which is a detail that I, as a woman, could understand. If I had been stronger, if I had been braver, I would have noticed how we were both not happily married to career-driven men; I would have recognized the same tired look we both wore behind our expensive makeup and fancy dresses; I would have appreciated the beauty that is friendship as our children played together; and, sadly, I would have realized I had lost the opportunity to create a new friendship of my own. These things made us more similar than different, and I felt terrible for not acknowledging her truth earlier. To make it worse, I felt like a shitty friend. That was the truth—my truth I wasn't willing to admit—and I couldn't help her until I faced that. I still see her from time to time, and while I've never told her what I realized at that dinner, each time Eyes-Maker has approached me, I avert my own in order to send a clear, nonverbal "eyes off" message. It is the least I can do to honor both of us.

Today I write about this because I know I am not the only woman who has been in this situation. It is a shameful moment of my being human that I've chosen to share because to maintain the "good" often comes with a furious inner battle, and that battle can last for years if we continue to be scared of the truth. Truth is never achievable as long as we choose temporary fulfillment over the long-term permanence of integrity. And integrity is the only way to protect our future, female or not.

To my current tribe of loving, truth-seeking women (and men who love these women); to my future shy, loud, talkative, and awkward friends; to the sisters who look at my clothes and makeup before seeing my soul; to the mothers who silently judge themselves as I once talked about my choice to breastfeed rather than bottle-feed; to the women who maintain "resting bitch faces" as a way to protect themselves from my naive search for rainbows and unicorns; to the sad, depressed friends who feel like they are "too much," who are impenetrably strong for my sake . . . please know I see you. I see you, and your crown is always straight and shiny and sparkly. And if it is to ever tip over, I will be there with bobby pins and hairspray (that's what dance moms do!), and we will walk out of the shitty bathroom of life together into the world without anyone ever knowing it needed fixing. Your truth is safe with me, because in the end, it is my truth too.

Have you ever fixed another woman's crown without telling the world it was crooked? #LunchNotes

(39) #SideBySide

JULIETTE JOYCE, PHD
SCIENTIST & RESEARCHER

When we are mistreated at the workplace, we often choose to stay silent. We feel alone, hopeless, and defeated. We are afraid that no one understands, believes, or supports us. We feel awkward to explain the situation to others, not to mention asking for help. However, all of us are both needy and needed at certain points of our lives. We need to accept the idea that it is okay to be not okay, and it is okay to ask for help.

When adversities happen, if we have a friend or a support group to walk side by side with us, our heavy burden will be lightened, and our spirits will be lifted up. In the meantime, when our friends need a helping hand or a listening ear, we can sit or walk side by side with them through listening, comforting, encouraging, sharing our experiences, praying, and taking actions.

Many books have talked about those coping and helping strategies. What I want to emphasize here is the importance of *side by side*. Being side by side means being present at every step of the coping, recovery, and growth processes. Being side by side means taking approaches that are tailored to help each other on to each stage of the journey.

In the initial stage, a listening ear might be all we need. After giving some thoughts about the situation, we might want to seek or offer some advice. It is not uncommon for some cases to progress to contentious litigations. In those cases, being side by side means that we can help with allocating effective legal services, being a source of strength and support, and accompanying our friends to go through the difficult and intimidating process. At this stage, a lot of uncertainty and stress is inevitable. Having someone at our side whom we trust and who has our best interest in mind becomes very critical.

My dear friend kept checking on how my children and I were doing when I had to fight to protect my children from their absent and abusive father. She thoughtfully squeezed her schedule to meet me at least once a week to comfort, encourage, and empower me. She listened to my struggles and offered her best advice. She accompanied me to the court on the hearing day to face the monster. She generously shared her wisdom, strength, and time with me. She supported me wholeheartedly to fight the good fight for my children. Without her side by side with me, I simply could not walk through the long, dark valley and survive.

If you are—and we all are—in need of such a wonderful friend or support group to be side by side with you, we are here for you! Remember, it is so true that the presence of the right person changes everything even if the circumstances do not.

We are better together.

Share your story of being supported or supporting others during difficult times. #LunchNotes

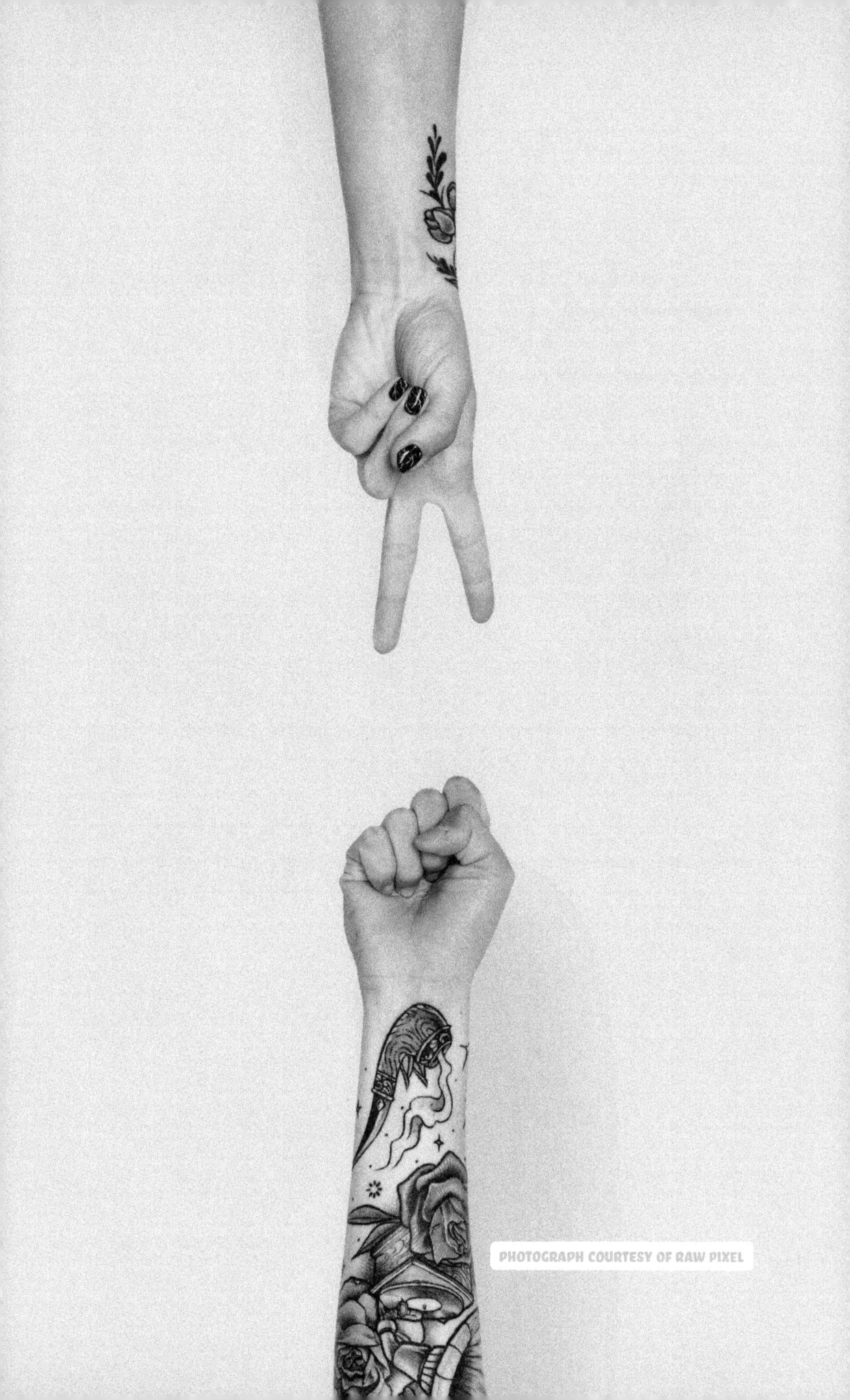

PHOTOGRAPH COURTESY OF RAW PIXEL

(40) #EngageToWin

If you choose to battle with the glass ceiling, I recommend that you engage to win.

To make this choice is a very difficult one, as embracing your stereotypes and social norms is the path of least resistance.

If you choose to engage, my advice is to engage to win. I'm sure no one decides to engage to lose or engage to give up halfway. Unfortunately, I have seen many women engage with much gusto, only to give up at the first sign of a scraped knee or damaged ego. If you choose to engage in battle with the glass ceiling, be prepared to get a knee scraped, earn a black eye, and possibly lose a limb.

You will not come out without battle scars. It is inevitable. Yet each scar represents a triumph over adversity. Adversity builds character and confidence to take down your next opponent.

My recommendation to the women of the modern world is to not shy away from adversity. Adversity typically has two possible outcomes: (1) it turns you into a bitter, angry person, or (2) it has the potential to create growth.

I have refused to let negative experience turn me into a bitter, angry person or let it define me. Instead, I used each experience to drive me toward growth. Turning each moment of adversity into a positive experience is key to ensuring growth.

Describe a time when you made the decision to engage to win. #LunchNotes

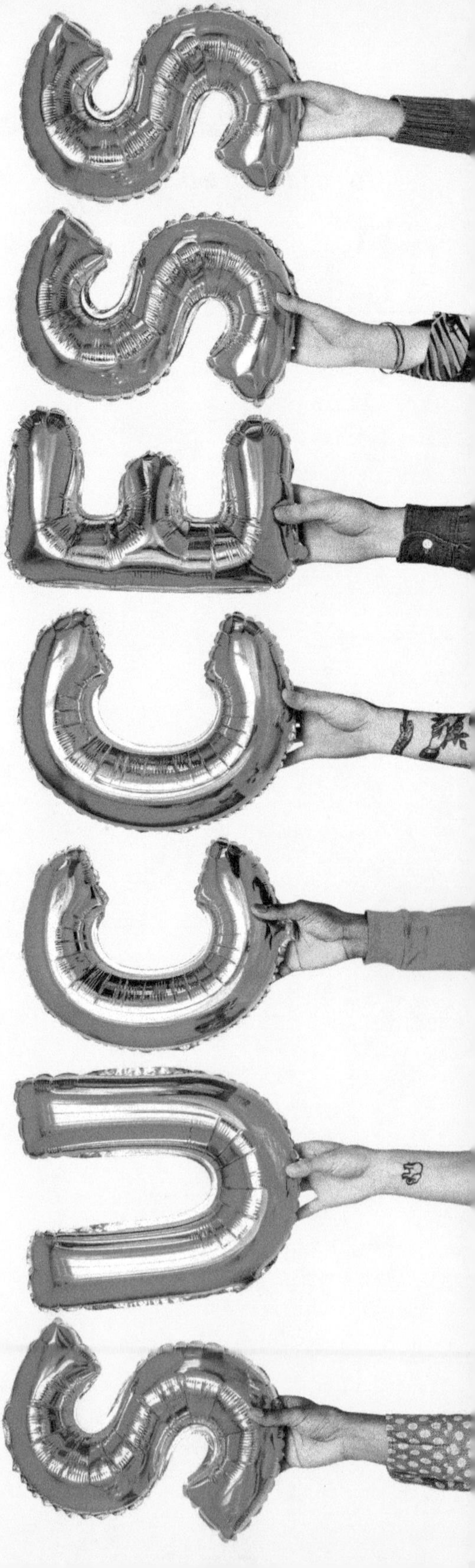

PHOTOGRAPH COURTESY OF RAW PIXEL

(41) #7S

As I go through my toolbox of hammers, battery-powered drills, and high-powered lasers to try to crack the acrylic-glass ceiling (a.k.a. asserting my ideas in the workplace), I have found that my toolbox of the Seven S's has been particularly helpful in getting clarity about my ideas, as well as ensuring the vitality of the projects.

I will share them with you in hopes that you can also benefit from the Seven S's.

- **Science:** Regardless of your topic, your science must be sound and water tight. Your ideas are stronger if based on data and scientific evidence. There is science to whatever field you are in. Whether it is interior design, marketing, gardening, personal training, or bench lab work. Understanding your subject-matter expertise is critical to your professional success. In every profession, there is an element of science.
- **Strategy:** If you fail to plan, then you plan to fail. Strategy is critical. This could include marketing your ideas at conferences, gaining exposure, and making sure you have support from below and above.
- **Sex appeal:** I don't mean cleavage. I mean your work must be sexy. It cannot be stale, overdone, and beige. There needs to be sex appeal oozing from the work. It needs to beckon for people to learn more and pay attention to every little detail. Like the curved lines on a high-end car, the body of the car needs to match what is under the hood.
- **Story:** This is incredibly powerful. If you can attach a story to your science and product, people will perk up, pay attention, and remember it. Remember, people remember not what was said but rather what they felt. For example, I often use my son for the inspiration of my work. Knowing his story allows my

audience to understand the humanity and reason behind my work.

- **Support:** Having support from all your colleagues, coworkers, family, friends, and leadership keeps your idea's flame going and ensures the project flourishes. You will lose steam at beat-down points of your life. This is when your support group will come in and hand you a power bar and a double espresso, to perk you back up so you can continue down your path.
- **Sales:** Marketing yourself, your ideas, and your brand is critical for success. Oftentimes, I see women close their office doors and hunker down with their work for the day. I recommend not imitating a weather-forecasting groundhog, only surfacing on a rare occasion to check if it is spring yet. Women often prefer to not get involved in office politics and fail to understand the temperature of the water. However, how can you engage in the game to win if no one knows who you are? Having one ear to the ground is critical to know when high-visibility projects are available, thus providing an opportunity to show off your talents and skills. Networking is critical for success. Meetings are created to *meet*.
- **Sponsorship:** Mentorship is different than sponsorship (please see #Mentors for more information). Those in leadership positions who are willing to sponsor your ideas and help pull you up from the mud are critical. It is imperative that you understand what your leadership wants and needs and that you provide what they are looking for. Learning how your leadership best communicates and investing time into understanding their unmet needs is time well invested.

  I have found sponsorship to be one of the most valuable assets for career development. In today's fast-paced society, we have less and less time for traditional mentoring, such as regularly scheduled meetings with a mentor. Rather, my meetings with my sponsors (which have happened without an official title and often organically) have been short and all action-oriented (meaning that after a few minutes there has been a direct action-oriented outcome, either the execution of an idea or a recommendation for a promotion).

Sponsorships can catalyze a career. Beyond offering advice and guidance, as a traditional mentor may provide, sponsors are advocates and connect you to key people, jobs, and assignments.

Since sponsors put their own reputations on the line when they advocate for you, it is challenging to find a sponsor. Leaders will typically give their time, attention, and relationship capital only to people who perform exceptionally well, or in whom they see promise in their character, work ethic, and personality.

Please share additional success strategies at #LunchNotes.

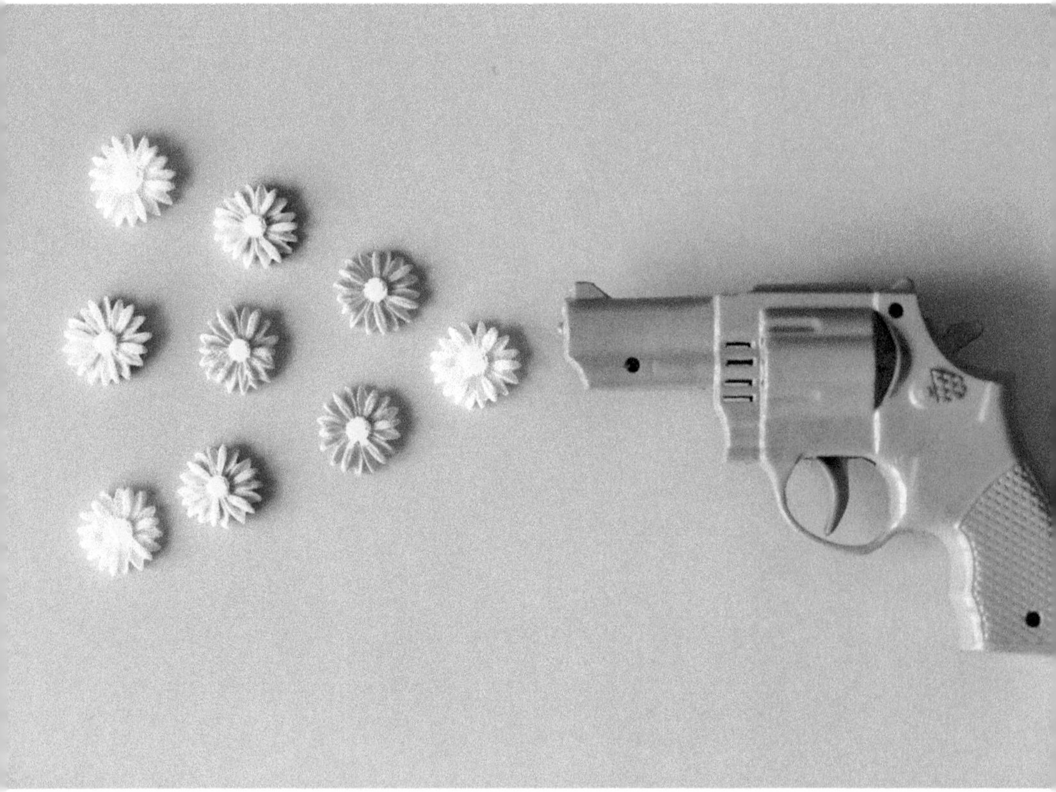

PHOTOGRAPH COURTESY OF RAW PIXEL

(42) #WomanUp

Making the decision to stand up for myself was an incredibly hard choice to make. This is probably one of the most challenging and difficult decisions a woman makes in her professional life.

I have relied on girly charms in the past to negotiate what I needed. This included using adoring eyes, smiles, and ego pampering. However, the day came when I decided that I no longer wanted to rely on these girlish tools and that I should woman up to fight for my career and stand up for myself. There comes a time in everyone's life when running away is not an option, as you will leave behind your work products, your network, and everything that you have built up.

I did not make this decision independently; I relied on the strength around me to help. My parents, husband, mentors, and friends all were rooting for me to woman up and to crush it. This was incredibly hard for me to do, as the scared little girl was still inside me, and I could hear her quivering voice, encouraging me to run away and hide. However, I knew that I could not turn away, as that little girl no longer defined who I was, and I knew that as a woman, I had the courage and strength to confront my adversity and solve my problems.

Describe the time when you decided to woman up at #LunchNotes.

(43) #BeAwesome

JULIETTE JOYCE, PHD
SCIENTIST & RESEARCHER

When we were young, we had dreams, and we completely believed that we were awesome in every way. However, after many years with our heads barely above the water, we have lost our confidence. We no longer believe in ourselves. We don't even think that we can be the best. We lost our dreams and hopes at work, after years of celebrating others' achievements and promotions; seeing our great ideas and innovations being put aside, ignored, or stolen; and tolerating our credits being taken or robbed.

All of these chronic negative experiences took a toll on our self-image and belief system. We are forced to accept the unjust treatments, ignorance, and ill comments. We don't believe in ourselves anymore. We doubt our intelligence, our ability, and our value. Gradually, we took in what others said about us, and this is very dangerous.

Ladies, we can be awesome, as we used to believe we were. And being awesome is the best approach to woman up and face many life challenges and problems.

My son has been blessed with a great friend. They spend almost every minute together at school. They invite each other to their homes and on trips when school is out. Obviously, they really enjoy each other's friendship and company. One day, my son said that he wished that he and his friend can stay best friends forever. I asked him if he knows how to make this happen. He thought for a while and said, "I want to be an awesome person and an awesome friend to him forever, and hopefully that will work." I applaud my son's insight, with which I completely agree. To be awesome may be the only effective approach in many situations.

Be awesome. Always be the best of ourselves, regardless of whom we are working with, what situations we are in, and where we are. Real gold is not afraid of the melting pot. Adversity and mistreatment cannot define who we are or restrain us from being our best selves, but rather refine us to be the best of ourselves. Being awesome at all times is who we are and what we stand for. Pure gold does not rust.

It takes time, effort, commitment, patience, self-discipline, and faith to be awesome. Invest in yourself. Sharpen your saw. Never stop learning. Sign yourself up for some continuing education programs to advance your expertise in your field. Read some books. Attend conferences or workshops. Feed your soul. Be sure to take care of yourself physically, emotionally, and professionally. Surround yourself with positive people and friends who support you or whom you admire. Build up strong and lasting friendships. Spend less time with coworkers who are always negative and not productive. Learn from people who are trying to be the best, most awesome versions of themselves. Be a source of positivity for those friends as well.

Lunch Notes

What are your approaches to be awesome even when you walk the valleys of life? #LunchNotes

(44) #FinishingWell

JULIETTE JOYCE, PHD
SCIENTIST & RESEARCHER

I can't count how many times I have felt defeated at work and at life in general. Many great ideas of mine sparkled and were developed into formal proposals; feasibility was assessed and confirmed; project teams were formed; excitement and enthusiasm were in the air; then the projects got killed with or without any reason explained. Sometimes it was because senior management preferred to give the opportunity to their favorite people; sometimes it was because someone didn't trust that an Asian woman was capable of carrying out a massive project, although I do have two doctorates and years of experience packed in my pocket; sometimes it was truly my "fault" because the methods I was proposing were too advanced for most people to adopt.

It is easy to start to doubt oneself and the value of those ideas and projects after years of being rejected and denied approval. As a result, we often give up and fail to push those ideas or projects through. It is funny that my coworker's office door has a sign that says, *Persistence is futile.* I dare not ask her how her experience has been and how she came up with this slogan.

However, I encourage everyone to persevere and finish well.

Due to various reasons, we often fail to reach to the finish line even though we started well. Throughout years of failure, I have learned some valuable lessons and identified some barriers, some of which I can overcome and some of which are out of my control.

One of the barriers for me to succeed is my accent. Although people are often very kind and accepting, knowing that English is my second language, it does get in the way when I try to convince an audience, especially when the topics are complex and innovative. To overcome this barrier, I made a commitment to squeeze in some private lessons to improve my accent and presentation skills when I was in my forties, which is a pretty late start. It was definitely not fun, but it was worth it. Gradually, my English-speaking skills have improved, and so has my confidence and the fate of my proposals, to some extent.

It is never too late to finish what we have started, and there is always a chance to finish well. Be persistent and be hopeful. Take your time, stay dedicated, commit yourself, and make an effort. Finishing well requires daily deliberate decisions.

Lastly, but importantly, finishing well requires teamwork. We are better together. Bear another's burden. We finish better if we finish together.

Do you have a story to share about how you pushed for something important to you? #LunchNotes

PHOTOGRAPH COURTESY OF RAW PIXEL

(45) #HealthyLikeABoss

MEGAN COREY
CERTIFIED HEALTH COACH & WELLNESS EXPERT

We all wake up in the morning excited to get out of bed, with a smile on our face, shouting, "Hello, world! I'm ready to take on my day!" Wait, what do you mean that doesn't happen to you? I see everyone posting this on social media with a coffee cup in their hands, sitting by the ocean at sunrise with their morning paper, or meditating in a quiet room in their house. So, this all sounds amazing, and I would love to have that at least one of my mornings each week, but let's face it—that's not how it is for the majority of the population. I'm used to hearing the alarm go off and peeling my eyes open to give myself a pep talk to go work out before the kids wake up and before work—that's if I even make it to the alarm, and one of my fine little rug rats hasn't decided that Mommy's bed is way more comfortable than theirs and tapped my face a few times to wake me up and scoot me over.

This is real life, people. We are trying to get our exercise in, raise a family, have a career, have great relationships, and then somehow fit sleep into all of this. When you read a book or a headline that says, "You can have it all, and this is how you do it," don't believe that shit. You can sure as hell have it all, but the way one person may do it will absolutely, positively not be the same for the next. Live for your life, not someone else's. Comparing will take you down a rabbit hole, where you will find not cute and cuddly Thumper but possibly a swarm of red fire ants. Yep, that's right, I'm telling you to get your ass in gear and go out there and do something for you!

What does it mean to you to live the best possible life that you can? Is it feeling good, looking good, success in all its forms, happiness, fulfilling your purpose, or maybe all of these? Psychological factors may influence health, which ultimately provides a better outlook on your mental and physical well-being, and there are ways to adjust your thinking and your habits to get you that fulfilled life that we all need and freaking deserve.

Your lifestyle and habits will lead you to your best self—even if you have gotten dragged into the trap of putting others first before yourself literally twenty-four hours a day, not only because that's in your nature, but also because you may feel guilty if you don't. Think about how much of a better person you are when you start taking care of you, when you are your best self and have a zest for life. Not only are you going to be feeling amazing, but everyone around you will feel that passionate energy that you are putting out there, and they will be better people in return. I always think, if everyone in the world was healthy and felt good, no aches and pains, stress free, how much better would our world be? We would be more considerate. We would smile and say good morning instead of having our heads down and focused only on our phone or our destination. We would allow someone to scoot in front of us on the highway in traffic instead of saying a few choice words, shaking our fists, and stepping on the gas. Seems simple enough to get here, right? Well, this takes some serious thought, dedication, and mindfulness.

Reducing stress and getting more sleep, both of which are two huge components of living a healthy life, get tougher and tougher as the demands of our families and careers take off. How do we change this constant circle of stress, anxiety, sleep deprivation, and body aches that lead to anger and resentment and decreased motivation? I'm sorry to say there isn't a right answer, but—yes, there is a *but*—the answer is right if it works for you and fits your lifestyle.

Let's take it a few steps at a time and walk through a few ways you can increase your lust for life, on your terms.

First, read some of the questions below, and write out your answers so you can view your results and have a baseline to start from.

1. Prioritize and write out your goals. What are you missing or longing for in your life that you have been searching for?
2. Once you have some targets in mind, ask: What does it take to get there? What do you need to fulfill those targets?

3. Assess your energy level and motivation. Do you wake up every morning as soon as your alarm goes off, ready for action? Or do you hit snooze twenty times, still feel like you are sleeping when you drive to work, then fall asleep on the couch when you get home?
4. Are you moving during the day? I don't mean doing a high-intensity interval training workout and SoulCycle every day, but I mean doing what works for you and what your body needs.
5. Do you feel satisfied with how you are eating, knowing you are putting whole, unprocessed, organic foods into your body and eating primarily home-cooked meals? Or do you feel like you want to take a nap or use the bathroom as soon as you eat something that may not be doing your body any favors?
6. Are you in a happy relationship, whether married, dating, or just having an amazing tribe of trustworthy, loyal friends?
7. Are you happy with your career and finances? Are you doing something you love, and are you motivated and fulfilled each day you are going to work? Or are you just collecting a paycheck and going through the motions because changing the constant is terrifying and risky?
8. Are you focusing on you and practicing self-care on a continuous basis, or do you feel guilty about taking time for yourself when your family or your job needs you at all times?

So, what do your answers look like? Did you take them and burn them with the cigar you just lit up from having to write this out, or did this open your eyes to see what areas you are totally getting an A+ in—while with the others, you wouldn't even want to bring home that assignment for your parents to sign? Well, you're in luck. There are ways to address these areas and work toward your best self. Writing out your goals and visualizing them takes some practice and then realistic expectations on how to achieve them. Don't think trying the new slim-in-five-hours diet or getting Kim K's butt by twerking all day is going to do it either. You have to establish and then prioritize how you want to address these areas to get you to lead that amazing life you want. Don't be so hard on yourself. Setbacks are opportunities for self-awareness.

What changes have you made in your life to create the healthy lifestyle that keeps you energized and motivated to push through each day? #LunchNotes

(46) #SleepNoise

MEGAN COREY
(CERTIFIED HEALTH COACH, WELLNESS EXPERT)

Sleep—it's is one of the most important things in your life that you need in order to be successful at all of the other things you want to do. Just keep repeating this phrase: If you can recharge your body, you can redefine success. You can! The most important way to recharge is to sleep. Sleep helps your body heal, reduces stress, and allows you to think more clearly to make the best decisions. Poor sleep can impact your nutritional choices and have you reaching for a Snickers over those carrot sticks. If you make this a habit, poor sleep can lead to an increase in cortisol, your stress hormone, leaving you with a tight fuse when dealing with stressful situations and ultimately affecting your metabolic function, which can lead to increased weight gain and fatigue.

But I don't think I've met anyone who says they feel as though they get enough restful sleep each night and feel amazing and ready to take on the day in the morning. We have so much on our minds and so much work we are trying to fit in that it's taking us longer to fall asleep, and then once we do, we may be woken up throughout the night by thoughts, pets, kids, or other noises outside of our control. What the heck are we supposed to do to get our sleep back so we can function and not be requested to audition for a role as a zombie in an upcoming movie?

Let's work on a few ways we can try to make this happen for you so you can get the rest of your life in order and conquer each day. Now, don't go crazy and think you will go from getting five hours of sleep a night to ten, and then if you don't, you just lie there awake, staring at the ceiling, and then give up. There could be several reasons why your sleep is compromised; this includes what and when you are eating and drinking, where you are sleeping, and how much energy you have expended throughout the day.

Start keeping a food journal to see what's going into your body and when, and see if something that you've eaten is affecting your sleep. Same goes for your bedroom. Is there clutter that is driving you bonkers? Put it away or throw it away so you aren't looking at it and stressing about it. Do you have dark blinds, a temperature-controlled room where you aren't sweating each night, and a comfortable bed? Now, think about what you've done today in terms of movement. Did you take the stairs all day at work and exercise and feel ready to sleep, or did you sit at home or at your desk all day with a pretty slim energy output, making you making you feel less sleepy? We can fix this. Start small and adjust as needed.

- Try to push your bedtime thirty minutes earlier every week.
- Try to limit what you are eating ninety minutes before bed.
- Reduce TV and phone time, which could be eating into your sleep schedule.
- Get a meditation app and listen to that to help you fall asleep and also get some meditation in at the same time! I'm all about twofers here, getting the most bang for your buck.

Is your mind whizzing with a never-ending to-do list of things you wanted to do today and didn't, as well as things you need to do tomorrow, put on the calendar, or tell your significant other? Journal or at least jot down everything that is going through that active brain of yours so you can fall asleep without worrying and pick up where you left off, more rejuvenated and more full of energy and ideas to complete that to-do list. Exercise is a huge factor in helping you fall asleep and stay asleep. When you get those stress-releasing endorphins on with your sweat workout that day, your body will truly feel more tired and ready to take that rest.

Are you woken by sleep noise? Whether it is snoring or street sounds, invest in a good white-noise machine and some silicone ear plugs to drown out the extra noise. I'm an extremely light sleeper, but using these devices has helped me fall asleep and not be woken up by these noises, and the plus side is I can still hear a crying kid when they are calling for me. On to the crying kid or pets: I know it's amazing to have that snuggle time in the middle of the night with your child, but sometimes it is in the best interest for you both to sleep in your own beds. There are obvious circumstances where having your child in your bed is necessary, but that habit will have both of you waking up throughout the night, which makes you both more tired in the morning. Same with pets. Have they taken over your bed with their size or their snores? Maybe it's time to have them in their own bed next to you.

Again, if sleep is a priority in your life, and you know this is something that is so necessary to make the rest of you function properly, try some of the recommendations above to get you set up for success.

How have you tried to adjust your sleeping schedule to make sure you are getting that much-needed quality sleep for your mind and body? #LunchNotes

PHOTOGRAPH COURTESY OF RAW PIXEL

(47) #TakeABreath

MEGAN COREY
CERTIFIED HEALTH COACH & WELLNESS EXPERT

Okay, I know what you're thinking: *I breathe all day long. What is this supposed to mean?* Well, how often are you mindful and conscious of the breaths you are taking? Do you ever take a minute or two to stop what you may be doing if you are feeling stressed, anxious, or panicked, and just take a few slow, deep, calming breaths to get yourself level set? Breath work is a free way for you to de-stress, reduce panic attacks, reduce anxiety, improve blood circulation, improve your mental state, and promote relaxation. Wow—who would have thought breathing could do all of this? There's a reason why yoga and meditation have such a following and why they are so good for you—in part because you are taking time out to do something for yourself, but also because of the mindful breathing that comes along with it and the benefits to your body that it brings.

Here's a quick breathing exercise developed by Dr. Andrew Weil that you can literally do anywhere, in your car to or from work, sitting at your desk in the office, prepping for a big meeting, or any time you feel like things may be spiraling out of your control and you need to become more in tune with your body. There are several breathing techniques out there to use, but this one is specific to relaxing breathing. Feel free to check out his website (listed in the footnotes)[43] and many others out there on hundreds of free YouTube videos and apps where you can follow along on guided breathing exercises.

43 Andrew Weil. "Breathing Exercises: Three To Try | 4-7-8 Breath | Andrew Weil, M.D." DrWeil.com. January 07, 2019. Accessed April 18, 2019. https://www.drweil.com/health-wellness/body-mind-spirit/stress-anxiety/breathing-three-exercises/.

The 4-7-8 (or Relaxing Breath) Exercise

This exercise requires you to sit up straight and plant your feet on the ground. You need to put your tongue against the roof of your mouth and exhale around your tongue, which will make a swooshing sound. After closing your mouth, inhale through your nose as you mentally count to four. Then count to seven as you hold your breath. Next, exhale around your tongue again for a count of eight. These steps are counted as one breath. You can repeat the above process for four breaths.

Did you try it? How do you feel? Now, everyone may feel different, but find something that works for you in terms of mindful breathing and put it to work for you. It's truly amazing how pausing and thinking about breathing can put you at ease in different situations, clear your mind, and allow you to focus a bit better. Start incorporating this into your everyday lifestyle. It doesn't take any money or equipment to do this, just you! So next time you are in traffic, cursing the car next to you, instead of screaming, getting red in the face, and stressing yourself out over something you can't control, take some deep breaths, put on a guided meditation (please keep your eyes open if you are driving), and enjoy your commute for once. This is also great practice if you are having a stressful day at work, then come home to a crazy house of little people who are ready to be fed but also cranky from their long day. Lots and lots of focused breathing. Get your kids to do this with you. It keeps them focused on their breath, too, which in turn calms their minds for a bit. If everyone took a pause to breathe before proceeding onto something they felt angry or stressed about, we may just create a less hostile work environment and a happier place to be living in.

What have you noticed from taking a pause each day to do mindful, deep-breathing exercises? #LunchNotes

(48) #GirlTribe

MEGAN COREY
CERTIFIED HEALTH COACH & WELLNESS EXPERT

Your tribe is your soul sisters or brothers who are there for you no matter what. You surround yourself with others whom you trust and who support or push you to be your best self. Does this sound like you, or do you feel like there are people in your life who are always putting you down or commenting on your little wins in a negative fashion? Start figuring out the answers to these questions: Who are the supporters in your life? Who makes you happy when you are around them? Whom can you trust? Who gives you valuable opinions and recommendations coming from a place of good and not jealousy? It's time to start filtering your tribe and creating more space for your relationships. Go for the quality of the people you have in your life, not the quantity.

The universe hates a vacuum. When we free up space in our lives, that area will automatically fill in with people, places, or things that align better with our vision. Consider the question: What person, place, or thing in my life is depleting me rather than energizing me? Write down anything that comes to mind. Choose one thing to release in order to create space and come up with a tangible action step to do so. Enjoy freeing up space in your life and moving in the direction of living in your highest alignment. Remove people who don't believe in you and find those who do. What friends can you count on, and what relationships can you count on? The universe sends in new people who are on a new level. Let them in, and don't be afraid to let go of your past. Your past is over. The only place it exists is in your mind. Be in the present and be in your future; be in alignment with the future you want to create for yourself. The universe will align with you. As it wants you helping people and making the world a better place, so it will help you. Things happen and come together that you couldn't imagine.

Putting yourself out there for things to happen is the hard part. Not everyone is motivated to chat with strangers or go to a networking event where they don't know anyone or stop by a happy hour to meet neighbors you normally just say hi to on the street. Many are comfortable with the friends they've had since grade school and are afraid to trust or let anyone else in. As Jim Rohn says, "You are the average of the five people you spend the most time with." Think about who that is. Are these five people truly your positive influence, and are they motivated in their lives as well? Or are they content with what's comfortable, coloring in the lines, doing the same thing day in and day out, not looking to try out new things, because the normal day-to-day is okay to them? It may be time to open up your circle and find those who are going to get you to where you want to be. Break out of comfort and enjoy the ride with these new cheerleaders, because they were sent to you for a reason. Give them what they give you and support and motivate each other to be a better person each day, and doing this only increases the chances of us contributing to a more positive universe!

Who is your tribe, and how do they lift you up and support you through all of life's ups and downs? #LunchNotes

(49) #EmbraceYourself

MEGAN COREY
CERTIFIED HEALTH COACH & WELLNESS EXPERT

Love yourself. Love what you are. Love your uniqueness. Embrace all of the qualities that you have that are yours and yours alone. Live each day the way you want to live. Make decisions based on your thoughts, aspirations, desires, and needs, not on anyone else's. Accept your flaws, your quirkiness, and your differences, and you will enjoy yourself, as well as those around you, so much more. People want to be around you because of who you are. You make them laugh. You educate them. You motivate them. You are a shoulder to cry on, an ear that can listen, and a hug for support. Embrace all that you are and how you serve all of the people you come in contact with each day. Sometimes loving who you are or embracing your uniqueness is difficult.

Here are some things to try to incorporate into your life that will allow you time to accept yourself:

- Allow yourself to be a work in progress. You don't need to be on your A game twenty-four seven. Do the best you can, and let the things you can't control materialize organically. Laugh at your flaws, address them, and move on. Most of the time, if I'm making fun of one of my quirky behaviors, my friends are laughing right along with me. That's part of my uniqueness and what I am about. I don't want to change that.
- You know that song "Try Everything," by Shakira? I heard it on one of my kid's movies and was drawn to it because of the meaning. Why shouldn't you try everything, say yes to more things that get you out of your comfort zone, and embrace the fun and excitement you'll have?
- Forget the "imposter syndrome" that is now a thing because of social media. Just because someone else is doing it doesn't

mean you can't do it. If you want to dye your hair pink or pierce your belly button because it's something you've always wanted to do, but you don't because of what people may think or because someone you know may have just done something similar, *do it*. Stop caring about what others may think about you, and do what feels good to you; and if they think you are copying them in some manner, just inform them that copying is a form of flattery . . . so there.

- Take some time out for self-care to truly thank your body and mind for keeping you alive and healthy. For allowing you to run and play with your kids, for being able to go to a well-paying job every day, to have someone who loves you for all that you are. Schedule that massage appointment for yourself, go to the library to read a book by yourself, take a yoga class, go to coffee with a friend. It doesn't matter how elaborate it is—just take that time for yourself to thank you for who you are. Your body and mind will thank you for giving it that much-needed break and time out.

Everyone was put on this earth for a reason. Embrace that you are here, embrace all that you are, and start fulfilling your purpose with what you were given. The uniqueness you not only inherited but have developed throughout your life isn't an accident. Use those qualities that are in you to love yourself and give love in turn to others.

How have you included self-care and self-love in your life, and how has that made you feel? #LunchNotes

(50) #Momfidence

MEGAN COREY
CERTIFIED HEALTH COACH & WELLNESS EXPERT

If you are a mom and you are out there day in and day out hustling to support your family, all while doing it with style and grace, or at least standing up, you are showing your momfidence. Growing up and worrying about myself and then going on to worry about kids was a complete game changer. No longer could I stay out until 2 a.m. partying with my friends and sleeping in the next day, run to Target at my leisure and browse the store for things I may or may not need, take time to make an extensive meal that required hours in the kitchen, and go to the gym for two hours for an amazing workout. Nope, times have changed. But you know what? I have too, and not in a bad way.

Once I became a mom, things definitely shifted from taking care of me and my friends and husband to now being in charge of caring for these two tiny humans. I adjusted to this different life and adjusted my priorities as well. To say your life is not your own once you become a mom has some backing to it, but why cave into some form of life that a typical mom should be living? What works for you may not work for anyone you surround yourself with, and that's okay. Try not to compare your life to theirs, and live it as only you can do, based on what works for your family.

Your life road map should be based on alignment to your goals as well as your family's, but don't lose sight of who you are in the process. Who says you can't still exercise, make a meal, go out for a drink with a friend, or get what you need from the store when you need it? Here's something to think about: How can you do all of these things while having a career and raising a family, while also making sure you are making time for your spouse or significant other? Well, I'm not going to tell you it's easy, because that's a lie, but it is possible.

It's possible if you prioritize the things that give you the most meaning, the things that are truly important to you and then make time for those things. You may not be able to do all of these things all the time, but start figuring out what you need to fulfill your life each day, and schedule that in. This makes the time for everything else to kind of fall into place. If you want to exercise, and that's important to you, try to get up before your kids do and before work. If you can't leave the house, set up a room in your house and do a free YouTube video. There are endless possibilities for free workouts at home. If you want to make more home-cooked meals and do meal prep to create a healthy-eating lifestyle for your family, find time to do this before your hectic week begins. Start saying no to some things that aren't serving you and your family at this time, and use that free Sunday to find a quick, healthy recipe or two to make so you now have three or four meals for the week and are less tempted to eat out. You need to get something from the store, whether it be groceries or batteries? Get it delivered. With Amazon and Instacart and all of the other delivery options, you can save yourself several hours a week by getting things delivered to your door. Find a recipe and order the exact ingredients so you are ready to roll by the time it's delivered. You want to make sure you have time to play with the kids and give them your undivided attention? Put away your phone, turn off the TV, and be present. Your mom guilt will subside if you know in your heart that you are absolutely present when you are with your kids, which will then allow you to do the other things that fulfill you without feeling like you are missing out.

Get your confidence back and think about who you were and what you enjoyed before you became a mom. Some of those things may not be what you want to do now that you are at a different place in your life, but if there are other things you enjoyed that fell to the wayside once you had kids, maybe it's time to look at these again. And, hey, some of those things may include the kids, which is a win-win for all of you.

What have you always wanted to do now that you are a mom that might be outside of your comfort zone, but that would give you the satisfaction of having and doing something for yourself outside of your normal mom life? #LunchNotes

(51) #ManInTheMirror

JASON WOO, MD
PHYSICIAN

Leadership and Self-Deception

How do we go about improving our work, our organizations, our lives? This is a question I have been working on for at least all of my thirty years as a healthcare provider and for more years before that, and I'm still working on it, even though I first heard Michael Jackson's song "Man in the Mirror" a very long time ago. Only recently have I begun to really understand the difference between creating change and creating meaningful impact.

Don't get me wrong—I certainly have my long list of achievements that I'm proud of and feel made a difference. But understanding why some of my strategies have worked while others have been less successful has puzzled me. I think I've been the same person, had the same values, used the newest techniques, and kept up to date on the latest process-improvement vernacular, methods, and recommended behaviors. Between W. Edwards Deming and Total Quality Management in the eighties, Peter Senge's *Fifth Discipline* in the nineties, John Kotter and *The Heart of Change* in the aughts, Six Sigma, Lean, the Theory of Constraints, and on and on, there always seems to be something new or different to try. Lots of recommendations on behaviors around communication, collaboration, creating vision and common goals . . . Sometimes they work for me, sometimes they don't, even though I pride myself on following instructions and techniques very well. Why don't they work?

What I have come to understand is that it is not the behavior you do or use that makes the difference in how others respond—it's how you view them. Put simply: Do I view others as objects that help, hinder, or are irrelevant to my objectives, or do I view others as people who have their own goals and objectives to achieve that matter to them like mine matter to me?

How is this relevant to this book? Well, when I think about being a minority or about times when I feel I've been discriminated against, or when I come up with reasons why I haven't gotten the success I wanted, I realize I've been putting myself "in the box," actually viewing myself as an object. I blame myself or others for not being good enough or failing to be accountable. This victim mentality justifies the feelings I have about the situation.

So, rather than accept the box that I put myself in or think that others see me in, if I open myself to the idea that others are just trying to be happy and valued, then it opens me to being curious about why they might view me in a certain way and to ask questions to better understand their whys. This relieves me of all the anxiety, anger, or negativity with the current situation and opens up a host of new information or options to consider in addressing what I think is my challenge.

This may not seem like an obvious answer to the emotions I may be immediately experiencing in response to what may very well be real injustice or discrimination. But what it does do is help me let go of those emotions and, in doing so, find the space I need to come up with a better response. As Viktor Frankl is credited with saying, "Between stimulus and response is a space. In that space is our power to choose our response. In our response lies our growth and our freedom."[44]

When I really ask myself this, I've realized that I've been most effective, happy, and at peace with outcomes when I view others as people *and* really make the effort to understand what they are trying to accomplish. Not that their goals or objectives are more important than mine, but I take the time and effort to understand what they are. In doing so, it's not just that I can find ways to align with them and be helpful, but that they probably feel me genuinely trying to be helpful. This is where the difference lies.

Most of us can probably tell when we are focused on our own goals, objectives, and needs. What we have a harder time seeing is when we

---

44 Viktor E. Frankl Quotes. BrainyQuote.com, BrainyMedia Inc, 2019. https://www.brainyquote.com/quotes/viktor_e_frankl_160380, accessed April 20, 2019.

think we are trying to be helpful to someone else or their needs or even what we think are universal truths, but we aren't really trying—what we might term an outwardly nice, inwardly focused mindset (i.e., I do for someone else what I think they want or need without really knowing if that's what they truly want). Why does that make a difference? Because it affects the way we go about interacting with that other person. When I think I am being helpful because of what I try to do, I am deceiving myself about what I am really trying to do—that is, *my* objective to be seen as helpful. This is part of the self-deception, and it makes all the difference in how I then respond to that other person and how I go about achieving my goals. When I don't get the response or outcome I expect and blame someone else for being the problem, then my self-deception becomes even more complete and self-justifying.

This is and is not an obvious concept. The more I've explored it, the more nuances I found to it that I can apply in my everyday life. Like many insights in leadership and self-improvement, though, my understanding of this doesn't itself make me a better leader or person. I find that continuing to be open to how I can learn more about others, understanding where they are coming from and where they want to go, and then considering how I go about achieving my goals in a way that aligns with their interests and needs is a continuous opportunity, yet it also makes me more alive to all those around me and the broader opportunities in life. Instead of barriers to goals, I see more opportunities and possibilities.

When I see life as not about what I want but rather about what and whom I can influence, then it's really much simpler to try to just understand others better, seeing their humanity and seeing how I can be better. It's no longer about applying the right strategy, behavior, or technique. It's just about finding my better self. It's a simple concept, though it can be hard in practice. The power is in the progress.

What tools do you use to help you focus on progressing? #LunchNotes

(52) #Introspection

RAJU RAYAVARAPU, PHD
SCIENTIST & RESEARCHER

When my sister and I were growing up, we weren't perfect. In fact, we were far from it. In retrospect, there have been so many moments from my childhood that must have caused my parents so much stress and grief. Our parents never spanked us or yelled at us, but they did participate in unconventional psychological warfare.

The biggest fear we had as kids was disappointing our parents. When we made a mistake, we didn't get yelled at. Our father would wear his disappointment on his face. To this day, I can picture it in my mind when I hear his voice on the phone. The genius of this approach was not rooted in their disappointment—every parent inevitably finds hundreds of moments when their kids surprise or shock them. The genius lay in the expectation that we had to figure out what we did and why it was wrong. For a six-year-old, it can be devastatingly difficult, but for an adult, this can be an invaluable skill that makes you a stronger, better member of society.

Most people know when they make a mistake. Betrayed by both biology and psychology, your mind races, your body sweats, and you might get nauseous. To reflect on your mistakes and understand them is a different animal entirely. People rarely see the real consequences of their actions. When you consider your actions as a whole, you are forced to consider their implications. What is frustrating and difficult as a child becomes a valuable skill as an adult.

Reflecting on our choices forces us to introspect. This helps us to understand our behavior and consequences. Frequently, we find that those who hurt us are unable to introspect themselves. They cannot understand how others feel, because they are unable to stop and look within themselves to understand how *they* feel. If you are unable to stand in your own shoes, how can you expect to walk a mile in another's?

Do you take time to self-reflect? #LunchNotes

(53) #DoWhatYouLove

Fun has always been a priority in my life. I've had the great fortune of rarely feeling like I was working for my paycheck. Although my journey has not been exactly smooth in recent years, I have enjoyed every curve, detour, and bump just because I have always been passionate about my work and made it a point to have fun. I consider every job as an opportunity to grow technically and creatively while overcoming new challenges.

Having the ability and mentality to find the positivity and meaning in my job has allowed me to perform at a higher level and motivated me to go the extra mile and produce a better product.

PHOTOGRAPH COURTESY OF RAW PIXEL

What do you love about your work? #LunchNotes

(54) #PowerlessToPowerful

KELLY SCOTT
OWNER OF FOREVER STRONG FITNESS

Of course, you want to be respected, capable, practical, and strong. While you can build those character traits in the classroom and the boardroom, you can also build them in the weight room. I'm here to inspire you to use strength training as a key component to your personal development.

My Relationship with Weightlifting

After I spent most of my twenties on and off crash diets and wrecking my metabolism, exercise had one of two purposes for me: to lose weight or to keep the weight off. What shallow purposes for such an amazing and constructive activity.

I'll admit, my initial purpose in lifting weights was to increase my metabolism by building leaner, more metabolically active muscle mass. Further research showed that the strongest lifts are the ones that require you to use more muscle groups at the same time and also burn more calories than training fewer muscle groups at a time. That's why I changed my focus from being a cardio junkie to being a lifter.

It was only after I switched to lifting like the boys did that I began to notice a more significant change to me. While an intense cardio session may leave you with a temporary endorphin high, it can also be exhausting and do little to make you feel empowered. In fact, the fatigue of post-cardio can leave you feeling vulnerable and weak.

You already know how important your health is to your success. Lifting weights will make you healthier. Strength training dramatically improves, or even reverses, bone loss. Strength training is effective in managing the chronic pain associated with arthritis and back problems. Progressive strength training also helps stave off cognitive declines and combats insulin resistance. It improves balance, coordination, and spatial awareness, reducing the risk of falls, and strength training can even extend your life.

Lifting heavy weights will build your character. What's better than feeling empowered? Feeling powerful? Being powerful? It's hard to feel insecure and uncertain about yourself and your place in this world when you've just finished a heavy training session. No woman ever walks out of the gym feeling defeated after hitting a personal best. Your head is up; you make eye contact; you walk with enthusiasm and exude confidence. It's not a show; it comes from within.

Even if you are having a bad day, when you finish your lifting session, you'll feel unstoppable. Depression fades, insecurity abates, and self-doubt disappears.

What Is Heavy Lifting?

I call *heavy lifting* any type of strength training in which you are focused on becoming physically stronger. Becoming stronger produces a tangible result that you can track. It's more than just a feeling. There are many ways to become stronger, and you can vary your focus of strength training for a well-rounded program. You can get stronger with just bodyweight training, but there's nothing like successfully picking up heavy metal objects and putting them back down without hurting yourself.

Barbells, kettlebells, dumbbells, or any other free weights you choose can have a powerful, transformative effect when you add them into your exercise routine. While they will all get you stronger, the techniques and body mechanics are different for each tool. So start with one of them, and master it. I'm a fan of kettlebells.

How to Get Started with Strength Training

Become a student of weightlifting techniques, and learn the proper technique from a qualified professional for the type of weight that you are training with. Approach your workouts with a purpose greater than burning calories. You are there to perform. Fitness is not defined by what your body looks like; it's what your body can do and how healthy it is.

Compound movements like deadlifts, pullups, weighted squats, and bench presses require more muscle groups and will definitely make you stronger than isolation movements alone like bicep curls, hamstring curls, or tricep extensions.

Once you've practiced the proper form and you feel confident in your movement quality, it's time to play with the big-girl weights. You don't need to become a power lifter, but using a respectable weight that requires you to brace your core in order to make the lift is the type of training that will get you strong. There is no magic number for how many sets and reps you should do, but you'll be able to physically demonstrate more strength if you are lifting in sets of lower reps. Anything in the three-to-eight range of reps per set will give you a magical high when you grind out those lifts with a respectable weight.

It will become addictive, and it will change the way you view yourself and the world around you. Tracking your progress and testing your strength periodically will keep you motivated and tell you when it's time to change things up a bit.

Who Wants to Be Weak? Not Me

Feeling weak is counterproductive to personal development. When you train with the purpose of becoming stronger, you begin to feel strong, look strong, and act strong. You become more decisive and certain in *all* of your actions. You become less timid and more assertive, and you ooze determination. You are what you practice. Make heavy weightlifting your practice, and you will be more likely to take on the heavy lifting required to climb to the top in life.

Strength-training movements may feel masculine at first. There are no sexy booty shakes or hip dance moves. I get it—cardio feels more feminine, and lifting feels more masculine. But if you are looking to level the gender playing field in life, it's all the more reason to join the strength club.

I've gone from feeling completely powerless in my life to inspiring and teaching others how to literally become powerful, strong, and confident. Your body, mind, and soul are not disconnected from each other. Training in one area has a direct carryover to the others.

Exercise serves a higher purpose than just improving cardiovascular health and staying trim. Many women avoid the type of exercise that will have the most dramatic effect on improving their self-esteem, body image, and confidence. So don't be afraid to do the heavy lifting. It will make you a more capable person and take you to where the strong people go.

No one regrets becoming healthy, fit, and strong. We only regret not doing it sooner.

When has physical strength translated into internal strength? #LunchNotes

(55) #GoldenBuddha

JESSIE KATES
OWNER OF SHIFT YOGA STUDIO

On a hilltop at a monastery in Thailand, there sat a massive clay statue of the Buddha. For decades he sat, stoic on the mountainside, adored and honored by everyone in town, until one day in 1957 when the monastery was being relocated and the monks were given the task of moving the massive statue. As they began their work, one of the monks noticed a crack in the strong clay facade, and he thought he saw a gold light shine back at him. Thinking he must be imagining things, he called over another monk and asked him to look into the crack, and he too could see the faintest glimmer of light shining back. Bewildered but curious, they began to chip away at the hard clay exterior, gently removing thick pieces of clay until they found beneath it the largest solid-gold statue of the Buddha. For years no one had seen the beauty that was hidden beneath the surface; the monks had long since forgotten it even existed.

This is much the way we forget about our own goodness. We too have forgotten that beneath the surface is a reservoir of peace and worthiness. All we see is clay. Historians believe that several hundred years earlier the monks had covered the golden Buddha with clay to protect it from an attack by the Burmese army

—much the way we cover over our own magic to protect ourselves as we flow through life and the joys and sorrows met along the way. We pile on layer upon layer of clay over the goodness in our own heart. We do this only to protect our innate goodness from being hurt by others and by challenging experiences until we, like the monks, forget it is even there. Many of us even go searching for it everywhere we can think of. We look for ways to change our lives, jobs, relationships, and circumstances, hoping that doing so will reveal our worth. But we must learn from the journey of the golden Buddha that worth lies within us. It might be tucked away under years of hurt, covered over by hardship and doubt, but eventually the surface cracks and our light shines through.

It is a natural desire to keep this precious part of ourselves safe. It is common to allow the experiences of the past, the hardships we endured, and the struggles we encountered to cover over our inner light. No matter what we have been through, we all have this golden Buddha within us. We all have an innate goodness, a divine inner light. We must rise above the past, peel off the layers of clay and hurt and wrongdoing, and step into the truth that has just been lying dormant, waiting to be rediscovered. You are a golden Buddha; you always have been. Peel off the clay and step back into your truth.

Lunch Notes

What is your truth? #LunchNotes

(56) #FeedYourSoul

MEGAN COREY
HEALTH COACH & WELLNESS EXPERT

What is your relationship with food? Do you get a headache just thinking about what you are going to eat that day or that week and how it's going to make you feel after? When you'll have time to make anything healthy or go to the grocery store? Or are you overwhelmed and unsure of where to even start in terms of what is good fuel for your body? We've all been there. It's completely overwhelming to even start to search through Pinterest for a recipe because you don't even know what to search for or know what is good for you.

Eating right doesn't have to be that hard, nor do you have to be a nutritionist to understand what is good or bad for you. With over 70 percent of our body's immune cells living in our gut, what you eat is a direct correlation to how you feel, staying healthy and reducing illness.[45] Listen to your body and how it feels when you are nourishing it with food and water. Follow your intuition about what is right for you and your body, not what might work for someone else, as everyone metabolizes food differently and food affects each of us in a different manner.

The simplest thing you can do when preparing meals for yourself and your family is remember to eat clean. Yes, I know it's the new buzzword for foodies and health fanatics across the globe, but if you think about it, clean eating is really just the act of eating whole, unprocessed foods that are as close to the source as possible. Eating clean revolves around maintaining a balanced and personalized diet of fresh, unprocessed food, including fruits, vegetables, whole grains, and healthy fats. It can also include eggs, meats, fish, and dairy. Taking this information into consideration, use organic at all times if possible. This is determined by the chemicals that are sprayed on the fruits and vegetables, as well as how your meat or dairy is raised and fed, with additional hormones added in. Besides the mental boost you get with eating clean,

45 Vighi G., et al. Allergy and the gastrointestinal system. Clin Exp Immuol 153(1), 3-6

some of the other positive effects are clearer skin, weight loss, increased energy, stronger hair and nails, improved mental health, and better sleep.[46] This isn't considered a diet; it's a sustainable lifestyle shift that you can include in your daily living without an enormous amount of effort.

Here are some tips for adjusting to this lifestyle change and making it easy on yourself to incorporate into your everyday existence.

- Eat as many whole, unprocessed foods as possible. If it comes in a premade package and has ingredients you can't pronounce, or if it's fast food and you are unsure of where the food has come from, it is processed food. If you are eating fresh fruits and vegetables, nuts, seeds, whole grains, grass-fed and free-range meat, dairy, and eggs, this is what whole food looks like.
- Try to cook your meals at home more often than going out to a restaurant. You know exactly what you are putting in your meal, and you are not getting all the additional junk that may get put into something from a restaurant.
- Limit refined carbohydrates, and aim to eat more whole grains. This means no white pasta, white bread, or white rice. Try out some new recipes using whole grains like quinoa, brown rice, or millet.
- Limit your sugar. The amount of sugar many people consume every day is leading to hormone imbalances, thyroid issues, inflammation, and weight gain. There is sugar in almost everything these days, especially processed foods. Try to reduce your intake little by little, and you won't have those cravings as often. If you need a little sweet treat, try some raw cacao or dark chocolate that is at least 70 percent dark cacao. You'll notice the sugars are a lot lower in the dark chocolate with a higher percentage of cacao than other chocolate bars.
- Best thing to remember: don't go crazy and stop eating everything for two weeks, get crazy cravings, and then eat everything

46 Vighi G., et al. Allergy and the gastrointestinal system. Clin Exp Immuol 153(1), 3-6

in sight and go back to where you started after that. Follow an eighty-twenty or ninety-ten rule. Eat as clean as possible 80 or 90 percent of the time, and then let yourself have some treats or alcohol or white pasta. I guarantee once you start eating clean, you will have fewer cravings for the bad stuff, you'll feel a whole hell of a lot better, and you will truly feel as though the things you do eat as treats are just that—treats— not something you need to have in your diet every day.

- Another major way to ease into the healthy lifestyle change of clean eating is practicing mindful eating: taking time to enjoy your food, chewing it, and letting it go through your body and nourish you before you reach for a helping of something else.
- Always remember to drink your water. Not only does water detoxify your system, clear up your skin, and fill you up, but it is so much better for you than a high-calorie, high-sugar drink. If you do have a craving, try to drink a glass of water and wait fifteen minutes. Your body may just be dehydrated and need to fuel up.

Start small and adjust as needed. As I mentioned earlier, start keeping a food journal and write out everything you are eating and drinking during the day, and note how you feel after. They say "everything in moderation" for a reason. Try everything so you aren't missing out, but keep it small. Look into the reason why you wanted to eat an entire cake yourself, scarf a huge bag of Doritos, or gulp down a gallon of soda. There may be something else that is leading you to using food as comfort. Once you have become aware of the cause, you can begin to set yourself up for success in eating clean!

MEGAN COREY
Speaker & Coach
megancorey.com

WEEKLY MEAL & SNACK PLANNER

MONTH

WEEK NO.

MONDAY

TUESDAY

WEDNESDAY

THURSDAY

FRIDAY

SATURDAY

SUNDAY

NOTES

What types of foods do you put into your body to nourish your mind and soul that make you feel amazing every day? #LunchNotes

PHOTOGRAPH COURTESY OF RAW PIXEL

(57) #ModernMan

I'm incredibly lucky to be married to a wonderfully supportive husband who chose to *modernize up*, instead of asking me to *regress down* to a role that I was not comfortable with.

As I was figuring out how to best navigate the modern woman's world, trying to avoid land mines and at the same time trying to support a healthy family life, my husband tested several methods of how to be the modern man, including learning to adjust to my needs and playing an equal role, not only as a loving and supportive husband but also as a highly engaged father. Learning how to communicate with me and respecting my career as a priority of mine were steadfast principles.

As in every partnership and friendship, the flexibility needed to adjust to the needs of your partner is critical. When my husband needs to travel, I adjust my work schedule to balance out the roles that he plays; when I need to work late, my husband fills in. We understand that it will not always be a fifty-fifty deal, as life is rarely balanced with two busy working parents. Sometimes it will be seventy-thirty; other times it may be forty-sixty. Regardless of the percentage, the meaningfulness of caring for our child and the fulfillment that we get from our marriage is always measured to infinity and beyond.

We share parenting duties not because we need to but because we love sharing in all the joys, challenges, and ups and downs of being a parent. We share in the joys and work because we each want to experience every part of parenting our beautiful child and because we want to grow in our relationship with each other.

Share a sweet moment when your life partner modernized up. #LunchNotes

PHOTOGRAPH COURTESY OF UNSPLASH

(58) #KindnessSeenAsWeakness

There have been many times when my kindness was seen as a weakness. This is a common occurrence to many people.

There are usually two types of reactions that ensue once someone has been burned by another who is using their kindness:

- The kind person turns evil and vows to never be kind to anyone again.
- The kind person maintains course and continues to be kind to others despite the negative experience.

Many may ask: Why continue to be kind to others when it can be perceived as a weakness?

The book *On Kindness*, by psychologist Adam Phillips and historian Barbara Taylor, examines this concept. Phillips and Taylor note that people choose kindness because they want meaning in their lives. Creation of new ideas, new ways of thinking, or meaningful work typically requires collaboration, and collaboration requires kindness—and transactions without the guarantee of reward. Those who find great joy in creation are willing to take the risk of being vulnerable, and they open themselves up to collaboration without the guarantee of a reward.

This is a type of mature kindness that goes beyond simple kindness. It's a full way of thinking. An adult who is kind, is kind principally because they want to foster a collaboration as a risky but necessary part of living a full human life. Kindness reinforces collaboration, and collaboration allows the creation of meaningful ideas that turn into meaningful projects that grow into meaningful outcomes and a fulfilled life.

When did kindness lead to collaboration and the creation of something greater than yourself? #LunchNotes

(59) #Mentor

If you have a mentor in your life, you are incredibly lucky.

If you don't have one, mentoring programs are a good place to start. However, my best mentor relationships were ones that formed organically with no formal conversation that they would be my mentor. The difference is similar to *asking* someone to be your friend rather than having the friendship form naturally and not forcing the relationship into a defined role. The two types of situations may lead you to a friendship. However, the first may feel forced and unnatural while the second may be stronger and more meaningful.

As I was wrestling with the glass ceiling, my parents were an incredible support. My dad told me that what I was going through was what every woman leader had gone through at some point in her life. And that was better training than any program that ended with a certificate in how to assert yourself and stand up for yourself.

He was right—not only that, but women leaders could immediately relate to what I was going through and wanted to support me. Relationships that were formed through my battle with the glass ceiling have been my most treasured relationships in my adult life. Support from leadership came not only as only emotional support and guidance but also as real, substantial movement to make things better for women in the workplace, enhanced with education, data, and training. My relationships with my mentors, men and women, have helped guide me through my career. They have provided support when needed, helped me avoid land mines, provided top cover, and pulled me up to stand next to them in times of adversity.

I have been fortunate to have access to a panel of mentors. My mentors have been those whom I could chat with over coffee about how-to best handle adversity and challenges, whom I could count on to advocate for me, and whom I knew would always be honest with me and tell me if I was heading down the wrong path. This panel of mentors has been extremely beneficial not just to my career but also to my mental well-being and my growth as a person.

The most beautiful aspect of mentors is that at some point in your life, you grow out of a mentoring relationship into a friendship. For example, you may outgrow your childhood martial arts instructor, who was a prominent mentor figure during your angsty teenage years, but you now have a wonderful friendship in your adult years.

Who are the mentors in your life? How have they enhanced your career choices? How have you enhanced their lives? #LunchNotes

PHOTOGRAPH COURTESY OF UNSPLASH

(60) #WarriorPrincess

During my adventure into womanhood and trying to navigate through our modern jungle, a very surprising thing happened. My husband fell deeper in love with me, and I with him. Our love story grew from chapter one (lustful, hormonal love) to chapter two (starting a family) and to chapter three (loving the people we have become). My husband found himself loving this woman I had become. He found this layer of femininity and strength within me incredibly sexy. He lovingly calls me his "warrior princess."

Through my battles, he would grip the bottom of his seat to prevent himself from taking a punch at the bullies or taking a machete to the glass ceiling himself. He knew that I needed to fight this battle my own way and that he was not playing on this field but rather on the sidelines, providing emotional support, listening to me venting night after night, providing hydration periodically, handing me a glass of chardonnay the moment I kicked off my shoes, and taking care of our son when I was too distracted or emotionally distraught to teach our beautiful child Common Core math.

This warrior princess fascinates him, and he loves me on a level that he didn't even know possible. He told me one night that he thought he loved when he met me, but he didn't know that he could love me this much. Through many battles with my adversary (the glass ceiling), the surprising side effect is that my growth during my time in the modern-day jungle, helped me form a stronger partnership and bond with my husband.

Share your love story at #LunchNotes.

Lunch Notes

COURTESY OF #ITWASNEVERADRESS

(61) #Shero

Forget about the hero in stories. The *shero* is the protagonist and common fixture in most of our lives. In our modern-day storytelling, the strong female lead is ever present. Women now depend less and less on waiting for their knight in shining armor to come and save them. The shero is ever present in today's working woman as we balance work, life, and kids, while at the same time holding a high-powered laser aimed at the acrylic-glass ceiling. We manage to navigate this modern jungle with incredible strength, grit, and power, to annihilate challenge after challenge.

Yes, we live in an era when superheroine strength is seen every day. Mental strength, emotional strength, and physical strength are seen at every level in the modern woman.

Sheroes, here we come!

Describe your shero moment at #LunchNotes

(62) #Cheerleaders

I find adversity is a great timesaver to screen out the fakes and haters in your life. Like a sieve, it quickly removes the impurities and leaves you only with the pure elements, like cheerleaders for your life.

During times of adversity, you can see into the core of those who surround you. The reality of your world becomes extremely transparent. This is rare, as most of the time you look at other people the way they want you to see them. There is typically a lack of transparency; people are cautious with what image they want you to see, and they hide their own secrets and true thoughts. However, during adversity, people's true personalities will be unwrapped, and you can catch glimpses into their personal agendas, insecurities, and natures. This is a rare opportunity to see beyond the superficial level of those around you, into their true souls.

One of the greatest blessings you can have is the experience of true support. This is incredibly powerful and empowering at the same time.

As you are running this marathon called life, having people on the sidelines rooting for you to succeed, cheering you on at times of stress, and providing resources (like water or energy bars)—believing that you can and will succeed—is one of the best parts of humanity. Sometimes, when you are struggling up a particularly steep hill in your marathon, having a friend run alongside you, coaching you on, can be the most important factor in whether you give up or persevere in the race.

This could be as simple as someone believing in you, standing by your side as you face the world, or it can be as profound as someone speaking out for you against a bully or your parents helping to take care of your children so you can get your life in order.

These people are your greatest cheerleaders, with pompoms in full force and Gatorade bottles primed to squirt in your mouth as you run forward with your game face on.

Who are the greatest cheerleaders in your life? Think of a time when your cheerleaders have provided support. Think of a time when you were someone else's greatest cheerleader. *#LunchNotes*

(63) #ModernDayPhilosopher

Busy. No time. Million things going on. These are the typical phrases that describe our everyday lives. We are often reacting to our lives instead of taking time to think about them.

We haven't had time to breathe and systematically think about our current state. I mean really think: going several layers deep to systematically break down the way society is set up, what we really want and to think about how to achieve what we need.

Often, as women, when we are faced with a fragile glass ceiling and are unable to break through, we internalize our failures and only share them with a confidant, with the caveat that they never reveal them. When we are harassed and put in uncomfortable situations, we confide in this confidant, and then most often we pack up our stuff and leave.

As such a pattern emerges whenever we are in a bad situation, instead of systematically finding a solution and organizing efforts to fix the problem, we often increase the secrecy around the problem and internalize it as our own failure.

Or if the situation is particularly bad or the abuse is particularly traumatic, we wait for our knight in shining armor to save us. But how are you sure that this knight will ever show up or doesn't show up to pillage your village? Sometimes you may be your best savior.

As our lives have increased in speed, and with the need to multitask and juggle household duties with work, we have had less and less time to think the way philosophers used to. In our modern-day society, philosophy is less appreciated than in the past. But I challenge us to take a moment and think on existential questions about the human condition. Challenge what is thought to be common sense or the normal way of life, ask questions, and re-examine the old ways of thinking.

Women should get comfortable inhabiting the austere, analytical world of philosophy, given that we have gained access to higher education. Philosophy is an area where men have traditionally dominated and distinguished themselves.

It is unfortunate, but in modern times, we have pushed philosophy to the margins as an academic exercise, neglecting the basic human need to find answers and seek the truth.

This book was created to facilitate modern-day systematic thinking—to form a highly influential system of thought and thus create change. Instead of feeling a whirlwind of emotion (anger, frustration, and so on), I challenge us to break down our feelings into logical ways of thinking. As we share in our thoughts, broken down by micro topic areas (each hashtag is a micro-thought), we can analyze where there are areas that can be addressed systematically. By systematically addressing the issues, we can build an understanding of the magnitude of each problem and of constant and pervasive issues and barriers, and we can see how they are hurting our society.

As you share your stories though the hashtag (#lunchnotes), we as a society will increase in our empathy toward each other and gain a deeper, more systematic understanding of our lives.

Instead of being reactive, we can be systematic in our thinking and behaviors to drive for greater positive change. By using philosophical tools of higher reasoning, we can understand how we experience the world.

We are the thinkers of modern times, integrating everyday concerns into the concept of philosophy—partly abstract, partly practical. We have the ability to systematically shape our futures, instead of internalizing our failures and waiting for our knight in shining armor to save us. When we have time to slow down and the space to think, we can ask questions about life, the universe, and everything as it relates to right now and engage in healthy, vibrant discussions on the topics.

The best thing in our modern day is the ability to share in our growth. Through shared experiences, we can share strategies, increase our understanding of and empathy for each other, and share an empowered future together.

Our goal is to continue conversations, bring awareness to topics, and raise these important issues to the surface. By bringing people together in shared experiences, we want to show that you are not alone and give significance to your experiences, as well as collectively provide shared strategies as we grow together in this awakening.

We welcome all experiences and stories. Share with us 😊

Hashtag

#LUNCHNOTES

Website

WWW.LUNCHNOTES-PROFESSIONALWOMAN.COM/

Facebook

WWW.FACEBOOK.COM/LUNCH-NOTES-FOR-THE-PROFESSIONAL-WOMAN

Instagram

WWW.INSTAGRAM.COM/NOTESLUNCH/

Email

LUNCHNOTESPW@YAHOO.COM

Did we miss any topics that we should have more discussions in?

Please let us know at #LunchNotes.

CPSIA information can be obtained
at www.ICGtesting.com
Printed in the USA
LVHW072209070120
642877LV00025B/1509/P

9 780578 509334